BOOK OF ITZOLIN

LIFE AND WORKS OF

ITZOLIN VALDEMAR GARCÍA

EDITED BY MIA KIRSI STAGEBERG

BOOK OF ITZOLIN

LIFE AND WORKS OF

ITZOLIN VALDEMAR GARCÍA

EDITED BY MIA KIRSI STAGEBERG

TARSAL PRESS ℮ SAN FRANCISCO

BOOK OF ITZOLIN
ISBN: 978-0-578-82076-7
First Edition

TARSAL PRESS

Phoenix Hotel originally published 2005
by Itzolinworks, a division of Silver Bay Books

Face Hanging Like a Star originally published 2007
by Itzolinworks

Published in the United States by Tarsal Press
A division of Silver Bay Books
San Francisco, California
All rights reserved

Cover photo by Mia Kirsi Stageberg

Contents

Introduction to *Book of Itzolin*

Itzolin Valdemar García was born August 5, 1975 in San Antonio, Texas to Norwegian-American writer Mia Kirsi Stageberg and the late Chicano activist-poet Cecilio García-Camarillo. He began life in the ferment and inspiration of the Chicano Movimiento.

Itzolin thrived in an atmosphere of public sharing. Even as a baby, he loved to be brought to marches or to Floricanto events with hours of poetry and song. At age three, he asked for the mike during a huge University of New Mexico literary event. Bemused, the emcee said yes, and Itzolin delivered a fiery speech in Spanish, with apocalyptic images of planets, shooting stars and cosmic battles. *"¡Y por fin la Gran Víbora se levantó y comió el sol!"*/And at last the Giant Viper rose up and ate the sun!

His father published several chapbooks Itzolin wrote and illustrated as a young child. Since his native language was Spanish, by his parents' agreement, he did not begin to learn English until he was four.

Itzolin grew up belonging to the community of *Danzantes*, dancers in the Aztec spiritual tradition in which he was baptized. At seven, he traveled with his dance troupe to Mexico City and, during a sacred festival, was allowed to lead La Danza Del Sol. He executed the steps flawlessly.

From early school years, he acted in the group La Compañía de Teatro de Albuquerque. He also performed throughout New Mexico in a group with his mother and two-year-old sister Cielo, who had a speaking part. Itzolin was a regular cast member of public radio station KUNM's "Radio Free Children." During studio recording, baby sister Oraibi Karina stayed quiet in their mother's arms, fascinated.

When Itzolin was seven, his father and mother separated, and a few years later she moved to Washington, D.C. There he studied at Duke Ellington School of the Arts. Passionate about storytelling through visual imagery, he wanted to become a comic book artist. A year later, envisioning a life on his own terms, he returned to Albuquerque and dropped out of school.

Itzolin moved to San Francisco, where his mother had relocated, and wrote his novella *Face Hanging Like a Star.* He then returned to high school and continued on to Yale with an Andrew W. Mellon Fellowship for Humanistic Studies.

He graduated from Yale 1998 with a B.A. in English Literature with Distinction and was awarded Best Senior Essay in Literature for "City of Liquid," his study on Juan Felipe Herrera. His graduate studies at Duke University and Stanford were funded by the Ford Foundation.

Itzolin was a poet, multitalented in art and music. His friends included writers, theater professionals, martial artists, activists and academics, cleaning women and janitors, revolutionaries and muralists, flamenco guitarists, exotic dancers, bodybuilders, filmmakers, foreign exchange students, and seekers of any age, nation or discipline. At Stanford, he had strong friendships with fellow activists. He also connected deeply with young San Francisco Asian writers and musicians in San Francisco and San Jose.

Itzolin often spoke for the unrecognized and the dispossessed. In 2003 he was completing his first manuscript of poetry, *Phoenix Hotel.* His imagery, often Latino or indigenous, sometimes Asian, moves through sacred and profane territory, switching between street talk and elegant experimentation.

Itzolin struggled passionately over his own identity, from gender to what it could mean to be an artist, Latino inheritor of Movimiento activism, soulful thinker and lover of humankind.

To follow Itzolin's twenty-seven-year lifespan, start with the timeline, "My Name Means Volcano" on page I. Then begin again with his baptism and continue through pictures, early writings, memories of some people close to him, and his final works.

He died tragically May 2, 2003. The gifts of imagination that he left us remain.

Note From the Editor

Book of Itzolin is a kind of codex, like the ancient chronological records that highlight nodes of a story. Essentially, it's Codex Itzolin, revealing many of Itzolin's voices, images and ways of being. Many shared their memories of him. I curated the book because, as his mother, I'm the only living person who knew him through all the transformations. I hope this will lead to more publications by others.

Itzolin intended the poetry collection *Phoenix Hotel* as his legacy. He wrote several of these poems in Spanish, then translated them into English. The two versions, instead of an exact match, have flavorful differences.

The section "My Name Means Volcano" is an illustrated, seventeen-page timeline of his life, which I annotated. Images of Itzolin throughout the book are either family pictures or his own drawings, except as shown on the page or the list of illustrations. A few youthful writings and journal entries appear. He wrote his extraordinary novella *Face Hanging Like a Star* at sixteen.

The audiotape excerpts come from private cassette recordings he made about his life and thoughts, during a long solo drive from San Francisco to Albuquerque and back—a trip he apparently didn't reveal to anyone. He kept the tapes. In transcribing them and throughout this book, I changed a few names for privacy, except where he clearly named his friends to honor them.

Many who knew Itzolin at different times have said he seemed surrounded by light. This was true of him from the beginning.

I believe Itzolin would have wanted these parts of himself shown to you. Doing the work has been an intense, often otherworldly adventure that gave me joy, sorrow, and abundant insights. As though finding the way through a cave, torch in hand, I used what I know of his light to bring it to you.

—Mia Kirsi Stageberg

My Name Means Volcano

In Nahuatl, one of the languages of Itzolin's ancestors, Itz means obsidian, Olin means movement. He decided on its meaning for himself:

Itzolin quiere decir Volcán. [Itzolin means Volcano.]

—Itzolin Valdemar García, age three

With his father

1975 Born in San Antonio, Texas to writer Mia Kirsi Stageberg and poet-activist Cecilio García-Camarillo, their first child. Mia's son Stefan and daughters Kezia and Shifra live with them in an old rented house in the heart of the barrio. Cecilio and Mia work intensively on the seminal Chicano monthly journal *Caracol* that Cecilio launched during the Chicano Movimiento's fight for justice. Itzolin is baptized by Maestro Andrés Segura, a leader of Danza Azteca, in a Mexican indigenous rite with ancient roots.

1976 During the older children's summer visit to the girls' father in Denver, Mia injures her knee falling through the faulty bathroom floor of their house. Afterward, Cecilio, Mia and Itzolin stay with a Carmelite nun, awaiting government assistance for a better home. Kezia and Shifra's father, who opposes the girls growing up in San Antonio, does not allow them to return after their summer visit. Mia is heartbroken. *Caracol* staffer Susanna de la Torre supports her by helping to care for Itzolin mornings, so that Mia can continue working at Cecilio's side. The García-Camarillos secure a Section 8 rental home for the two boys, where Itzolin plays with pillbugs as favorite toys.

1977 Cecilio and Mia participate in the Texas Farmworkers March to the Capitol in Austin. Mia brings Itzolin in a stroller, and he responds with joy to the group energy. Artist Gloria Osuna arranges a co-op with Mia, Susanna de la Torre and others, each family caring for all the children one morning a week, so the women can continue their political work. Cecilio hopes to further his vision for the Southwest by moving to another city, and *Caracol* is passed on to Alfredo and Susanna de la Torre. Itzolin's parents bring him and Stefan to Albuquerque, initially staying in the basement of radical New Mexican land-grant activist Reyes López Tijerina. Family moves to a small rented garage apartment.

1978 Second Albuquerque move, to a bright, roomy apartment on Arno Street in the Martineztown quarter. Itzolin plays with a Mexican boy downstairs. He memorizes the names of dinosaurs and constantly draws them. Starts to learn Danza Azteca and takes to it eagerly. Sister Cielo Sirianna García born.

1979 Faced with a daunting rent increase, the family moves to an adobe house on Lovato Street in rural Albuquerque. Mia plants Mexican morning glories on an entire side of the house, and Cecilio creates a trellis from posts and string. At a public University of New Mexico event where poets perform for a huge outdoor crowd, Itzolin asks for the mike and declaims a spontaneous apocalyptic poem.

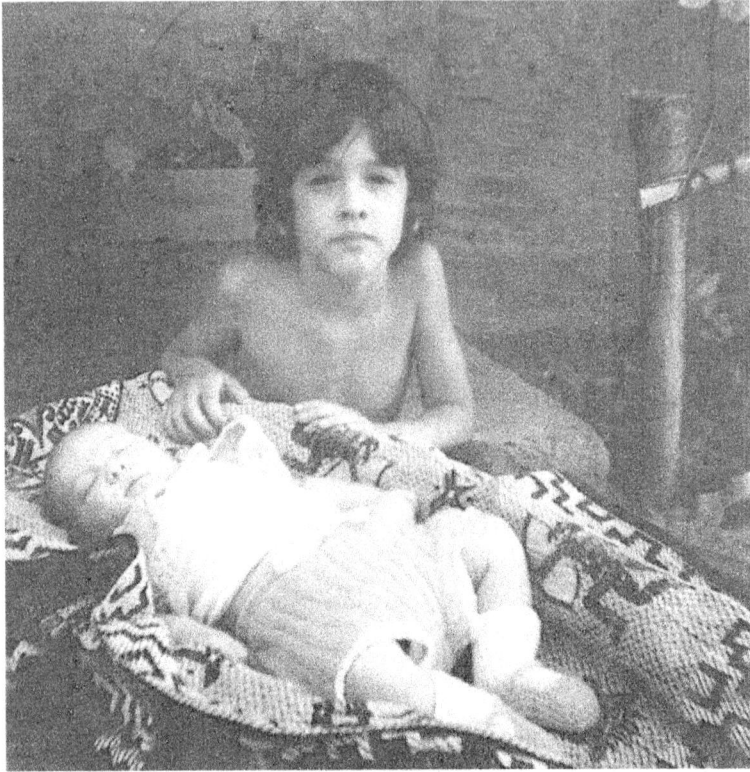

1980 Sister Oraibi Karina García born.

1981 Itzolin's constant companion is sister Cielo. They play beside Mia's vegetable garden and wander beyond to eat wild mulberries. Sisters Kezia and Shifra visit for the first time since he was a baby. Performs in a play at the Kimo Theater with La Compañia de Teatro, a professional community group. Also acts in theater troupe Corazoncitos del Pueblo, which Velia Silva and his mother have formed with their children. His drawings are featured in a calendar by local artists' group Taller Liberarte.

1982 Several illustrated booklets by him are translated from Spanish to English by his father and published by Cecilio's Muchos Charcos Press. The chapbook *El Volcán de La Dragona: The Dragon's Volcano*, one of Itzolin's spontaneous tales from a family poetry session, is illustrated with drawings he made at the age of five. *Una Mañana Extraña: A Strange Morning* is based on a dream told to his mother. *El Perro Fiero de la Acequia: The Fierce Dog From the Acequia* follows. As a member of traditional Aztec dance group Xinachtli, travels with them to Mexico and is permitted to perform La Danza Del Sol at the center of the circle.

Muchos Charcos Books
431 La Vega Road SW
Albuquerque, NM 87105

copyright (c) 1982 by Itzolin Valdemar García

Page from *Una Mañana Extraña*

Page from *El Volcán de la Dragona*

1983 – 1984 Itzolin's parents go separate ways. His mother moves to an outbuilding behind the house of close friend Lonni Ann Fredman, two blocks from his father, and the children live in both homes. Close friends include Nikko Harada, Greg Jackson, Yusuf DeMartino, Jane and Mindy Zhang, Nathaniel Goetz, and Sandro Quagnali-Lindsley. Fourth chapbook, *La Casa Del Brujo: The Sorcerer's House* published.

6.

En unos cuantos días se quebraron los huevos
y salieron los bebitos.
Ellos sabían donde estaba su mamá porque ellos
miraron a sus pies, y sus pies se miraban exacta-
mente a los pies de ella, nomás que los de ella
estaban más grandes.
Pues en unos poquitos días los bebitos
llegaron a la otra casa de la mamá dragona en el
volcán, y allí vivía Dios también.

*

In a few days the eggs cracked and the babies
came out.
They knew where their mother was because they
looked at their feet and their feet looked exactly
like their mother's feet except that her feet were
bigger.
Well, in a few days the babies went to another
house that belonged to the dragon mother. It was
in the volcano and God also lived there.

Page from *El Volcán de la Dragona*

8

1985 – 1986 Continues to act in plays with La Compañia and University of New Mexico's Experimental Theater. Practices breakdance and popping. Fifth chapbook, *Pepe el Piano,* published by his father. Article by columnist Dave Nordstrand in *Albuquerque Tribune,* "Kid Does More in Nine Years Than Most Do in Lifetime," includes lines from poem "What Is a Mother?" written when he feared to lose her to a critical pneumonia: "A mother's eyes are beautiful as rivers with mermaids splashing /A mother's ears are a tunnel where the water of life floats and where the snow queen rides her snow-white unicorn." Tells Nordstrand, "I already mainly know what I want to do for a living. I might be in theater or maybe an artist or a writer."

1987 Plays guitar. Takes martial arts lessons in Chan Wushu Kung Fu along with his mother. Because she struggles to make a living in Albuquerque, she relocates to Washington, D.C. with musician and acupuncturist Zhong Wingay and improves her work life. Cielo and Oraibi Karina join her. Itzolin takes figure drawing classes at the University of New Mexico. Planning to be with his mother in the coming year, Itzolin creates a portfolio to apply to Duke Ellington School of the Arts in Washington, D.C. and wins acceptance. Hopes to become a comic book artist.

1988 – 1989 Moves to Washington, D.C. to live with his mother and sister Cielo. Exuberant family nights and jam sessions with brother Stefan, above, who has also moved to D.C. Sisters Kezia and Shifra visit. Friends include Cathy Samper and a boy called Priest. The art school's training for exceptional students to develop professional careers pressures Itzolin physically and mentally, but he wins a Key Award for his drawings. Spends vacations writing fiction. Decides his future is not in visual art and moves back to Albuquerque with his father. Attends local public high school, which frustrates him. Writes his song "Maker of Rainbows."

1990 – 1991 Disaffected by school, he's suspended for playing the guitar in a school corridor, wearing a Native American necklace instead of a shirt. Instead of returning, drops out. Visits his mother and her boyfriend, Baltimore artist Neil Mick, at Vallecitos Artists' Retreat. Confides to his mother that for several years, a childhood mentor in Albuquerque has molested him. Mother files report with Albuquerque authorities. She and his father agree that when it can be arranged, Itzolin should live in California, where she's relocating with Mick.

1992 Moves to San Francisco. His mother is temporarily at home, recovering from a street attack with serious injuries, both wrists broken. Although it appears a random robbery, Itzolin worries it was committed by associates of the man who molested him. With his mother's support, spends several months building his energies and writing the novella *Face Hanging Like a Star.* After a summer job at Bernal Heights Neighborhood Center, returns to school in San Francisco at McAteer High, in the non-traditional Alta Program.

1993 Entire family travels to Cuba, New Mexico for his mother's fiftieth-birthday celebration. Youngest sister Oraibi Karina comes to San Francisco to live. Itzolin applies to five Ivy League Schools. Often stops by sister Shifra's Chinatown apartment to study. His mother continues to speak with Albuquerque police on charges against Itzolin's molester. Although Itzolin declines to testify at trial, the offender is sentenced to prison.

1994 Graduates from McAteer with top honors, wins scholarships to all schools he applied to, and chooses Yale.

1995 – 1998 Develops strong friendships at Yale, including Jeremy Tucker, Carlos Mena, and Benjamin Carp. Often visits brother Stefan in New York. Has first serious relationship, a young Iranian-Irish woman. Mentors include Dean Rick Chavolla, Director of the Native American Cultural Center and La Casa Cultural, and Professor Bryan J. Wolf in American Studies. At Yale commencement 1998, awarded Best Senior Essay in Literature. Graduates with Distinction.

1999 – 2001 Remains in New Haven another year, tutoring and bodybuilding. Moves to Durham, North Carolina for graduate school at Duke University, under an Andrew W. Mellon Fellowship. Close friendship with Juan Carlos Rodriguez. After his first year at Duke, his father is diagnosed with prostate cancer. The family pulls together. Takes leave to live with his father in Albuquerque and works with Southwest Network for Environmental and Economic Justice. On a visit to friends at Yale, meets the love of his life, a young Korean woman studying there. Back in Albuquerque, he's fraught by coping with his father's serious illness, the new long-distance love relationship, work life and writing. Suffers intense insomnia and flashbacks of molestation. His father encourages him to go back to school.

2002 Accepted to graduate school at Stanford University on a Ford Fellowship. He and his girlfriend move to San Francisco and rent an apartment in the Mission district. Works as apprentice locksmith in Chinatown through summer. At Stanford, studies with people he admires, such as the playwright and activist

15

Cherríe Moraga, filmmaker/theorist Fernando Birri, and others. Itzolin is deeply saddened when his lover leaves to resume studies at Yale. Becomes involved with El Centro Chicano and develops a close network of friends, including Eric Manolito, Gabriela Spears-Rico, Kuusela Hilo, Alfonso González, Jenny Lam, and Michelle Zamora, as well as Micaela Díaz-Sánchez and Lola Roibal whom he's known since childhood. Continues to live in San Francisco and stays close to his mother and sister Oraibi Karina (below) who live only a mile away, in the apartment where he spent hardworking high-school years.

His beloved father dies of cancer. Regretting that he followed his father's wishes that he go back to graduate school, begins to drink and intermittently use the antidepressant Paxil, prescribed by a therapist. In October, secretly drives to Albuquerque to visit his father's empty house. Has forgotten that the family removed the key from under front mat. Drives back to San Francisco. Writes in the Kearny Street workshops, first studying with with Truong Tran, then Edmond Chow. Forms strong friendships with community of young Asian artists, writers and musicians, attends the APAture festival, and participates in readings at Japantown venue Locus. Friends include Ishle Yee Park, Melanie Palermo, Jane Kim, Annie Koh, Nancy Hom, Michael Cheng, Stanley Lam, Kim Mizuhara, Robynn Takayama, Marilyn Yu, Gagan Palrecha, Debbie Yee, and Ravi Chandra. Itzolin compiles a collection of his poems, *Phoenix Hotel*, and gives copies to his mother and a few close friends.

2003   Writes elegy for memorial service of family friend he'd known since he was born, poet and activist Ronnie Burk. Burdened by societal expectations—academia, his father's political legacy, future student debt, and conflicts about biculturalism—he only wants to be a poet. Considers leaving the country or marrying a woman he's dated only a short time. Abruptly goes off Paxil medication and suffers sensations of insects crawling inside him. Mother urges immediate medical help. Visits a clinic, receives encouragement, gets new prescription and takes first capsule. Stays up late, agitated and drinking heavily. In the early hours of May 2, ends his life.

Baptism

The night Itzolin was born, Cecilio held my hand all through the intense labor. When our new son came, his arms and legs thrashed like wild pistons. Cecilio had to hold him while the nurse cut his umbilical cord. As my body shook from all we'd been through together, I knew this baby had a lot to do in life.

Cecilio and I had become fascinated with Nahuatl, the Aztec language that was part of his heritage. We had even run a contest in our journal *Caracol* for contestants to write poems in English, Spanish, and Nahuatl, all in the same poem. (We provided a list of fifty Nahuatl words.) This language could describe time, swift animals, and the sun—liltingly, yet infused with a piercing sense of nature's power. The name we gave Itzolin is Nahua, for his

Aztec ancestors. *Itz* means obsidian, that potent and mysterious black rock. And *Olin* (Ollin in Spanish) is the constant unfolding of creative energy that makes the universe and all of life. We used the Nahua pronunciation, Itz-O-lin.

His middle name, Valdemar, was for my grandfather Egekvist who had traveled from Denmark to Minnesota to make his way as a baker. His Egekvist Bakeries prospered throughout Minneapolis and St. Paul. Valdemar was a man of hard work, but also of reflection. Thin, straight-backed Itzolin looked a bit like him.

When Itzolin was a tiny baby, he was cheerful except for one time of day we called "the Hour of the Wolf." Around five in the evening he would howl, no matter what we did. He did not want to drink milk, be carried, have a clean diaper or a bath, hear music—it was maddening. One night as I sat with him. watching, I softly asked what troubled him. And I felt he thrashed his arms and legs as if he wanted to be free, I took away all his clothes. He stopped crying and smiled, as he lay moving his arms and legs..

When Itzolin was about six weeks old, Maestro Andrés Segura came from Mexico City to baptize him in the Aztec spiritual tradition. We had so much to do to get ready. In just a couple of days, Cecilio had to arrange a formal breakfast at a restaurant and buy cigars for the men, candy for the women, and toys for children. I had to make Itzolin a white garment like the Aztecs wore. It was made of two long rectangles, one passed between his legs and one round his waist, to make a loincloth. Then two white squares, one in front and the other in back, knotted at the shoulders as a tunic. I sewed these by hand from unbleached muslin. Articles like red corn, small clay bowls and paint had been brought from Mexico, and others had to be found quickly.

The night before, Cecilio, Andrés and a few other men we knew drove across San Antonio to make sure the baptism site had been planned well (it was in a park). I stayed up all night making the white clothes.

While it was still dark, I woke my daughters. We all drove to the park with members of Andrés Segura's dance troupe who had come with him from Mexico City. They had dressed ceremonially in beautiful colors—tunics, long skirts, feathered headdresses.

The places where each of us stood in the forest clearing were set by tradition. Andrés, in a state of high alertness, waited for the exact moment to start. I don't know how he knew. *Copal* incense smoldered, smoke bringing the distinctive odor from its amber chunks. We turned to the four directions and then up, down and center. Itzolin was passed from my arms to Cecilio's along a line of other people to Andrés. And then the sun began to rise. At the very moment Andrés held the naked baby up in his arms to the sun, its first strong ray broke on us all. Itzolin had been watching with eyes of intensity and odd joy. At the moment he was lifted up, a jet of urine from him spouted high in the air and landed on the imperturbable maestro. It was funny, but also sweet, as if he had to find a way to make his own statement about everything. Itzolin did not cry when he was bathed in cold water.

The maestro took special objects from a reed mat and held them up for Itzolin to see, one at a time: red Mexican corn, that he might love the land it came from. A little stick bound with a tuft of animal hair, like a brush. And tiny clay dishes of fresh red and black paint. These represented writing and painting, since in Aztec tradition they're the same, with important stories told by glyphs. We imagined Itzolin would be one to teach and write, inspire people, and fire their hearts with creativity and reverence.

Afterwards, we all stayed a while, laughing and talking quietly. I wrapped Itzolin in warm blankets. He murmured, waving his hands, and seemed absolutely happy.

—Mia Kirsi Stageberg
From memoir *Radiance and Cold Wind*

1975 Mia and Cecilio at a Floricanto

1975 Bathtime, San Antonio

1975 Sunshine

Bound volume of *Caracol*, which ran 1975 – 79

1975 With Mama, San Antonio

enchanted with the poetic qualities
of camarillos' baby boy Itzolin
eating up Gregory Corso's drawings
or Orphee strumming the harp
(itzolin nahua for movement like ringtailed tornado)
I know he's gonna fracture the zodiac
ceramic ashtray he keeps grabbing
like he cuts teeth
& glass tabletop he clobbers with a maraca

From "I Miss An Invitation to a Sufi Wedding
Visiting the Camarillos"

—by Ronnie Burk, in February, 1977 *Caracol*

1976 On the Texas Farmworkers' Marcha de los Campesinos

From the time of his birth, Itzolin was full of wonder. His strong little feet ran so swiftly I could hardly keep up, as he exclaimed over birds, red flowers, hurtling clouds, palm trees and pillbugs, pointing. "Mira Mami!"/Look, Mami. He often invented words. He called any tiny, fascinating, adorable thing a "kiki." At a year and a half, he pointed to himself and announced, "Ikiki!"

—Mia Kirsi Stageberg

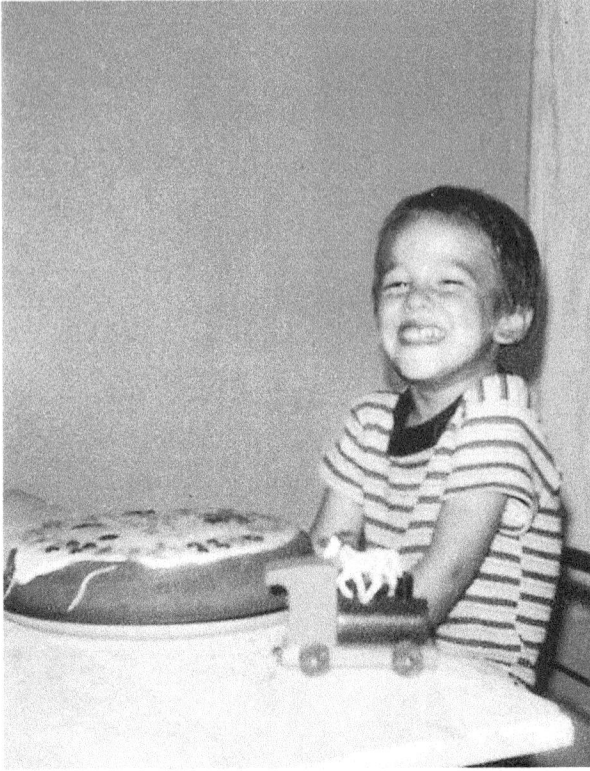

1978 Third birthday, Albuquerque, Martineztown

'UN CIEN-PIES'
POR ITZOLIN
AGOSTO 1979
4 AÑOS

1979 Centipede by Itzolin

1979 Our garden, by Itzolin, South Valley of Albuquerque

LO QUE ITZOLIN HACE EN LA MAÑANA:

1. SE LEVANTA
2. SALUDA A LA FAMILIA Y AL SOL
3. SE VISTE
4. RECOGE SUS PAJAMAS
5. COME
6. SE PEINA
7. LAVA LA CARA
8. SE LAVA LOS DIENTES
9. LES DA BESITOS A MAMI, CIELO Y ORAIBI
10. SE VA A LA ESCUELA

1980 Itzolin's morning schedule, by his mother

1980 Stefan and Itzolin, South Valley, Albuquerque

Names throughout his life:
Itzolin (Nahua accent, on middle syllable)
Itz-Ollin (Spanish spelling, Spanish accent on last syllable)
Mi Chapulín ('Buelita Julia)
Itzo (friends and family)
Tiko (family, close friends)
Olin (Yale)
Oly (mother's family)
Tito (friends and family)
Tilo (one of his jobs)
Itz (friends)

1980 Cielo, Papi and Itzolin, South Valley, Albuquerque

Pan de dulce.
Comemos un tipo de pan de dulce de Norge
que se llama Kavring.

Pasas.
Las pasas son una de las comidas favoritas
de Itzolin.

Pescadito.
Dice la abuelita, 'Tu eres mi pescadito'.

Paraguas. Cuando viene la lluvia,
 necesitamos una paraguas.

Pantuflas.  Aquí están las pantuflas
de abuelita.

Piña.

Plato.

Pirámide.

1980 Itzolin's diccionario, by his mother

1981 Dinosaurs by Itzolin

1981 Cucuy by Itzolin

1981 Caballos by Itzolin, from chapbook *Una Mañana Extraña*

1982 Preparing for Méjico with Xinachtli Aztec dancers

1982 Méjico, by Itzolin, age seven

When we were little, Papi would make *atole de arroz.* He never used very much honey but the raisins made it so sweet. My mouth watered at the sight of those plump raisins floating around in hot milk and rice. We had to split it between the three of us, so I would watch carefully as Papi separated the atole into three small bowls. I always prayed that I would get a bunch of raisins in my bowl. Somehow, Itzolin always got the most. He would inhale his atole in about 10 seconds, then eye my bowl and the raisins that I spooned off to the side. I wanted to save the best for last. But every time, I just saw him looking over and I could never say no to my big brother. I guess I always felt like he needed more than me. So, I would spoon every single one of my raisins into his bowl. He would just laugh and eat them all in one joyful bite. Itzolin's laugh was like music in my heart. I want to feel that place in his chest where my head fit perfectly when we hugged.

—Cielo Sirianna García (b. 1978 – d. 2018)

1984 School picture, Albuquerque

I was a friend of Itzolin's for twenty years or so. I remember
sleeping on his garage roof at his father's house, knocking
down bamboo with wooden swords to save the princess (his
sister) in his mother's backyard in ABQ. I remember role
playing games with our friend Yusuf, and teaching him
martial arts by having him do various outlandish feats. Even
through high school's usual drama about women and rebel-
lion and college's version of reality, I remember his goofy
smile always waiting for me. We would drive to the moun-
tains at night and talk for hours. The thing I remember
most was the light that surrounded him.

—Greg Jackson

And Life Begins—

By Itzolin, circa 1984, age 9

I slowly drift around in a spherical shape,
Forming a dazzling cloud of glittering colors,
I proudly spin and twirl.
Sparkling colors soar out into space.
I can feel myself being pulled in,
Being closed into a peaceful circle,
I link together, forming a hard ball.
Then I rotate,
In harmony with everything else.
Slowly,
Spark erupts,
Then a flicker and a whole spurt of flame,
I heat up to an incredible degree
Slowly, but surely, I begin to throw off the hot, flaky crust
From my back and shoulders.
I roll in glee
Pure
Holy
With amazing speed
I begin to quiver
Light shines out
I heat up
Swelling
Then—
I explode
Far, Far, everywhere, turned inside out.
I am free
Free to start new life.

The Skelsi

By Itzolin, circa 1985, age 10

It is sexually classified as tawrayell. This is generally equivalent to female, in our terms. It carries the orange egg cases in an unusual pocket near the base of the tail. This is specially designed to concentrate the body's heat onto the cases. Inside the pocket, there is a microscopic blade, made of several bodily chemicals, which pierces the single cell in the egg case, and splits it as many times as possible. This proceeds to create several offspring, from one cell. The tawrayell Skelsi goes on with normal life, until after about 3 months, it drops the egg cases, on the sand. The tawrayell protects cases from scavengers. In a period of about 5 minutes, the young split the case. They take large drinks of a fluid which drips from the tawrayell's sting, which induces a deep sleep. The young dig deep into the ground, go into a deep sleep, for up to 50 years. They involuntarily feed on the ground's nutrients. They develop fully, & then emerge, up to 13 feet long. To reproduce one Skelsi, there must be 3 types of Skelsi present. The rayell, which is similar to a dragon, fertilizes the eggs, which are supplied by the centillerees, and then incubated by the tawrayell.

We spent whole lifetimes up in the treeless treehouse at my house, carrying blankets and pillows up there, drinking iced Tummymint Tea out of a thermos, and gobbling books whole like goldfish crackers. Other days, sometimes near acequias, constructing epic plays where he was an Aztec feathered serpent warrior and I was a mysterious Samurai princess, or we were spies and carefully constructed ciphers and corresponding decoders out of paper rings and brad rivets. One year, after the Ice Cream Social at school, everyone broke up cardboard by the playground and brought them up to a room so that he could breakdance. That night he taught me how to poplock my tongue. I still do it. Later, in college, I remember passionate arguments, both telephonic and continued without pause in person while home on breaks, about single paragraphs of *Finnegan's Wake* or just sitting, side by side, in the backyard, largely quiet, interspersed with made-up constellations that both of us could see and nearly simultaneously named. There is one I still see, one we named and made ours, that Dragon-Amidst-Clouds that still hovers, sometimes, when it's entirely too hot, and there is not enough breeze, but I still feel him in the periphery, in the glittering night.

—Nikko Harada

1988 Subway with Cielo and Oraibi Karina, Washington, D.C.

1988 With his mother, Tidal Basin, Washington, D.C.

The Melting of Ymerr's Frost

By Itzolin, 1989, age 14

Often, when the deep dark sky is shaken by thunder, the people of Shurkhaan remember the dusky legends that tell of how the great frost was melted, and how the ice that gripped barren mountains sloughed away. They tell of how deep into the night, when the moon shone like the sun, only with blue light instead of the fiery red of the sun's rays, sharp cracks and booms shook the entire land with brutal force. Back then, of yore, only one race existed that was like man, and they knew of the origins, for they were close to the frozen caves of the frost trolls, and every night they were awakened by the ruckus which they created. Indeed a ruckus it was, for the troll children would smash rocks and shriek with glee. Not a soul on the planet of Totramesklaan was untouched by the chilling force behind the trolls' ferocity.

Not far from Totramesklaan were the shadowy forests of Khaalan, where the tree giants dwelt. They were a strange and grim race, the kindred of Jack in Irons, who came before. As tall as the tallest red trees he stood, even as he slouched, and about his waist was a belt of iron forged by dwarves below the ground. From his belt hung on chains the heads of many past trolls he had slain, for he hated their putrid souls.

As time passed, the beard of Jack in Irons became red as he aged, and he began to have children. None can say who was mother to these children, but some think it was the earth that bore them. His many sons and daughters were not as fierce as him though, and their arms, as strong as they were, did not sag so far below the waist. They bore offspring among themselves, and gradually grew smaller and smaller, for they were not half the height of their father. They were giants nonetheless, and so, like their allfather, they learned hatred for the trolls. They learned too of the mighty battle between Jack in Irons and Ymerr, whereupon

Jack in Irons had journeyed past Shurkhaan and even the mountains of Metiiken and Balkaan, to the home of the frost trolls. He had crushed their icy homes, for they had stolen many of his children, and he warned he would slaughter them all if they paid no heed.

Ymerr, the allfather of the trolls, had then come forth to battle him. For three days did they grip each other under their muscle-bound arms and box each other. But Jack in Irons was the stronger. He finally held Ymerr's monstrous body to the ground with his foot and made him swear that he would never again steal his children.

But as Jack in Irons strode away, Ymerr cursed all giantkind, swearing they would perish under the cold of winter. Jack in Irons only walked away, rumbling the earth with his giant footsteps. Ymerr was nearly as huge, and only someone like the allfather of the tree giants could have no fear of him. But the children of Jack in Irons had learned to fear the allfather of the cold and his fierce winters. Though they became strong and terrific when they battled the trolls, the cold made them weak.

Years went by, and Jack in Irons died, leaving his children to fend for themselves. The tree giants became less ferocious and strength began slowly ebbing from their colossal bodies. Often, the frost trolls would journey over the Balkaan mountains and come too close to Shurkhaan and Torwaak. The children of Jack in Irons would become angered as berserkers do, and run forth to meet them in battle. And though they would flail the trolls mercilessly, the trolls needed only to touch the giants and weaken them with the cold blood that flowed through their bodies, then kill them.

But amongst them was one that battled as fiercely as Jack in Irons himself, and he was small, only twice the size of a man. Og was his name, and upon his head was a metal cap, forged by his own mother. Fortunately for the trolls, he was unable to enter battle along with his kindred regularly, for his mother was ill, and Og cared for her extremely much. So he remained at home and nursed her back to health. He was restless; it was his sole desire to slaughter the trolls, and yet it was more important to renew his mother's health. The chilling cold was weakening her, and even as Og built fires to thaw out her bones in their lofty cabin and fed her broth, she remained unhealthy. Og became frustrated and then angry. Every day he would don his skullcap and imagine himself holding it high in the air, honoring his mother and allfather above the felled corpse of Ymerr.

Soon Og's mother became slightly better, and he was quite relieved, but as soon as her health returned she died. Og kneeled beside her as she spoke to him, and the last thing she told him was to never forget to give thanks to life. He made a promise, as his mother sighed her last breath, that he would thank life with his best effort, even if he joined his loving mother doing so.

Solemnly, he took his belongings: his skullcap, his loincloth, boots and furs, and built a funeral pyre for his mother. Og watched as she burned, a tear forming in his eye, knowing she was cold even as the fire flew her to the stars. He felt a burning inside his heart, an energy forming within him, and he felt not the cold.

Og knew what he must do. Og's mother had told him incredible tales by the light of the flame in their cabin, about the feats of Jack in Irons and of cruel Ymerr. But more importantly, she had told him of their allfather's bones. She was their caretaker, entrusted to keep them in a safe place. This place she had revealed to Og. He strode there, behind their cabin, digging up the earth to find the pyre of Jack in Irons. He then took as much bone as he could carry, for the bones of giants were like metal. He thanked life for such a gift. Then grimly, like one who prepares for war, he set forth on foot to hammer at the Dwarves' anvils. His mother had done the same before Og's birth, and therein was the belt of Jack in Irons forged; and he intended to find the door to the dank, underground tunnels for his own purposes.

Over land and sea did he travel, his anger pushing him further and further into unknown lands. His mother had recounted her journey to him only once, but he remembered her words and did his best to follow them. He walked and walked, taking long strides and swinging his thick arms with determination. Passing through the Totopakk swamps, he found many unpleasant situations, but he continued his journey, even as the humongous, deep green crocodiles that swam in from Ophmerr attacked him, and exceptionally ravenous creatures wrapped themselves about his iron-thewed legs and sucked his blood in the murk of the water. But it was not long before he had breached the broad, yellow fields his mother had told him would bring him to the door of the Dwarves' dwelling.

And indeed they did, for Og found a huge sullen toad squatting before him, and he knew it was near. Not without a struggle was he lent a hammer and anvil with which to work, for he found the hole in a magnificant old tree that led to the Dwarves' domain, but he was too massive to fit so much as an arm through the hole the Dwarves passed through by shapechanging into toads. Og knew not of any such magic. The Dwarves were reluctant to share their anvils when he called up to the entrances, and they glared at him with moody eyes. He explained his predicament and his oath to end the chill that was killing his folk. And the Dwarves agreed it was an important purpose, though they knew little of Ymerr and his frost, for they were warm in their furnace-filled tunnels. Nor did they truly give a fig for other folk or their conflicts.

But at last they lent him their appurtenances.

And so Og began hammering together the bones of Jack in Irons on the anvil, but soon found that the strength of his bones had crumbled the hammer and steel anvil. Feeling abashed and ashamed, Og did not request another set but removed his skull-cap and hammered the bones on it with his own fists.

Many years before, his mother had created the skullcap here, forging it with reverence and fierce intent, so that it was extremely perdurable and withstood the young giant's bludgeoning fists now. Og pummeled fiercely, working into the freezing night. The ground vibrated terribly as he worked, crafting the bone into resplendent shapes, and Og was interrupted by an annoyed toad who emerged from the thick-branched oak, only to behold the birth of a mighty armor, gleaming all white, shiny and stronger than the steel of swords.

But beholding the pulverized remains of the anvil, the Dwarf rose in height, attaining a squat form like a short human, and calling his brethren, he began to bicker with Og. But Og only lifted his gargantuan armor, fitting it on amid much clanging and snapping and angry shouts of protest from the Dwarves. He then knelt to the ground and gave his thanks to life before departing, and he also asked to be forgiven for crushing the precious tools of the Dwarves. The grey beards of the Dwarves trembled as they flew into wrath, but though they clung to Og and vituperated at him, they were flung away as he proceeded with his journey into the land of the frost trolls.

He moved with far more speed and determination than ever before, and it seemed that, as he walked the many miles over Totramesklaan's lands that were needed to reach Ymerr's realm, it grew colder. But Og did not become weaker; he waxed stronger. For as the days passed quickly, Og beheld himself expanding and climbing in height. He felt no fear, for he was preparing for battle, and he knew that his growth was the work of his fierce will and intent. Indeed he did expand and climb, for his eyes became like two hot coals, immune to the winter, and his hands began looking like the fangs of a spider, ready to close in on their prey. And too, it seemed as if the armor dissipated, molding about the iron ripples of his swelling flesh, and as his head began looking down a further distance to survey the earth, the armor truly appeared to be grafting with his skin. Og's purpose became so clear and distinguished that his mind was filled by it, and no other thoughts entered his consciousness.

Then, as another day passed that Og went without food or sleep, he saw that his strides were like that of his father, Jack in Irons, and his powerful arms were brazen like the layers of rock or a mountain slope. No longer was he small, no indeed, he had become mighty beyond words, and as he trudged on, his bare back gleaming in the light of sun and moon alike, with crevasses between his muscles like steep cliffs, the thunder of his footsteps shook the house of Ymerr as though he were right before it, striking its base with his feet.

Og came closer with every step, and Ymerr was roused by it. He pulled at his long, icy beard and clenched his teeth, for he felt the power behind the reverberating footsteps, and knew they were intended for him. So Ymerr began summoning the power of the frost, building, commanding it, and it obeyed him. Ymerr's bones were renewed by the chill, and his skin blanched white as ivory. He grinned, pleased as he foresaw the foe that approached kneeling before him, pleading for his life.

But as he saw Og striding forth in his swaggering lurch, like a towering mountain brought to life and unaffected by the cold, his smile fled, replaced by a look of terror. For, unlike Jack in Irons, who carried trophies of his battles, this giant bore only iron in his glowering eyes and titan thews, and Ymerr recognized it as the inevitable will of a man that would fulfill his purpose or die. But Og did not look as if he would die, and Ymerr felt horror and dread sink into his frozen heart. And before he realized it, Og was before him, plowing through the frost trolls. He felt the ground being pushed lower with each monstrous footfall beneath the giant's weight.

"I have awaited this moment for too long, Ymerr, allfather of the forest trolls, you who command the ice demons and harness their wrath. I know not how you have lived so long, not do I care. You have sickened my people, and there have been many insufferable deaths; for this I care. And for this vile deed, you must die. But I will spare you my ear, if any of your foul words are important now. Is there anything you wish to tell me ere I kill you, Ymerr?"

Ymerr turned to flee from that burning gaze and ear-splitting voice, winged by terror, but Og laughed so loud, it seemed as though Totramesklaan were splitting in half. He took Ymerr by the neck. "You cannot hide from me, feeble Ymerr, no matter how far you run." And at that, Ymerr thrust forth freezing hands to Og's neck, and squeezed with all of his strength, but he stared in fear at Og's unmoved face. Ymerr's terror swelled as Og tightened his own grip until he could no longer breathe.

But Og was not using his strength then as he did now, for in a single twist, he took Ymerr's head and ripped it from the neck. Ymerr's salty white blood gushed forth onto the snow, engulfing the frost trolls as their faces contorted with screams of horror. Og flung the skull towards the stronghold of ice wherein Ymerr had reigned, and watched the fortress shatter into millions of sporadic ice slivers.

And there he stood, until the sun declined past the snowy hill, and the bodies of the trolls floated in Ymerr's white blood like tiny boats in a sea. Og then knelt to his knee, and removing his

48

skullcap, he thanked life for allowing him to help his people and avenge his mother. And then, fitting on his skullcap once more, Og retrieved Ymerr's head from the ice and wrapped his snowy beard about his waist as a belt. As Og walked with his mighty stride, the cold and hoarfrost began melting.

And thus was Shurkhaan and Tomaak and all of Totramesklaan rid of Ymerr's curse eternally.

1989 Wild snow with Stefan and Cielo

Back in the 80s, when I was a bike messenger in D.C., on Friday evenings, after hanging with my buddies, I would often go to Mama's apartment on 16th street, across the street from Malcolm X park, bringing a pizza. Those evenings gave me some of my most treasured memories. Itzolin and I had this groove we developed where we would sit around the dinner table and sing Beatles songs. The idea was to go as over the top as possible, and imitate not only the vocals but the instrumental parts as well. This was especially fun with "Hey Jude" and "A Day in the Life" (with all the dissonant orchestral parts at the end). Itzo was always ready to goad me to the next level of absurdity, in the service, of course, of cracking up ourselves, Mama and Cielo and Karina.

One time, after a bone chilling and unreal snowy day (snow is surreal south of the Mason-Dixon line) I came over, needing more than my usual share of family warmth. Somehow, we (Mama, Cielo, Itzolin and me) went outside, Mama toting her camera, and Itzo barefoot. I don't think I will ever laugh harder than to see Itzolin prancing around in the snow, making a joyful spectacle, raising his naked foot covered with snow ridiculously high in the air so Mama could get the shot. I have that picture framed on my kitchen wall, and will cherish the moment always with all my heart for its inspired and crazy sanity.

The summer before, I'd had a serious accident on the bike in which I injured my head. Itzolin gave me three of his most prized belongings, two comic novels and Tolkien's *Lord of the Rings*, to ease the boredom of recovery.

Itzolin could speak the many languages of love and understanding with such clarity. Every fiber of my being tells me that his departure from life was a tragic mistake, and that though his road was intentionally dangerous and difficult, the mature, reflective happiness that lay before him would have helped make whole many others besides himself.

—Stefan Armstrong

1989 First day, Duke Ellington School of the Arts, D.C.

My Friends Were the Shadows

By Itzolin, 1990, age 15

My friends were shadows. I perceived the world only as light or dark, I spoke to the shadows as I would later understand to speak to people. I could always articulate words, but to utter them was a strain for me, and I found my nature in the corners where darkness pooled and I could converse with my friends. They were good, the shadows—faithful and kind, and full of wisdom, which they whispered along the breeze almost imperceptibly. The shadows had no names or identities. They were capable of coalescing into huge figures that it seemed could have masked the sun, and they could glide silently like clouds—they could scatter quickly and hide themselves. It was only seldom that they showed themselves to others in full, and I was one of those that won their trust.

It had always been my desire to be free, to scatter into corners or coalesce into such a huge mass that it could blot out any light. Why should I conform to the expectations people have of me? The whole truth is that all of the adults of this world have stolen from me. They stole from me by creating this dreadful society and bringing me into it. I have no place here—of all places, why this cesspool? But I was confined to a life of eating, sleeping, shitting and watching strange beings walk by. I had no solace from the bitterness that filled me. I could've reached down my throat to grab my pumping heart and I would've found nothing. There was only emptiness for me. I looked everywhere for cognizance of my problem, thinking I could understand and do away with it. But that only worsened things because I was forced to interact with adults. They were supposed to understand me, but instead they were baffled because I didn't conform to their image of a youngster. I got no help.

I had mighty questions as a young child, about God and the universe and sex and love. Adults, it seemed, were creatures that had abandoned creativity and spontaneity for a sheltered life in which there were no changes. Even at age seven, I was disgusted, and swore never to live in such a world. If I ever found myself in that situation, it would mean I had lost all convictions, integrity and self-reliance. I was a little boy so full of life that my eyes shimmered, and the human world was no place for me.

So I turned to the shadows. Leaping across walls and floors, painting surfaces dark, hiding in crevices and playing at night. I cursed the solid material world that held me and pummeled its gates, wailing to be let out. In the end it was the shadows that came to me out of sheer curiosity. Who was this strange creature pursuing them and imitating them? They wanted to know who I was, and we began to communicate. That was how it began.

I admired and loved them more than I did any human. There was so much that the shadows were capable of that made the human world a dreary place, and so the more I grew to enjoy the shadows and their profound world, the more I willingly withdrew from the odious world of humans. The shadows put on shows that satirized humans, silent monologues; they were brilliant pantomimes. When it was all over, the shadows would dance again, frolicking in alleyways and corners, in caves and dank basements. The shadows showed me everything they could—they performed wonderful things in front of my eyes and invited me to join them, and I was happier than I had conceived possible, and this seemed a start to a new life.

But the beauty of what I was living was not held into account when my fate was decided. Who makes the rules? I was dragged away by adults to an institution I learned was called school. I tried to explain that I didn't belong there, that I was a shadow, and couldn't they see what an error they were making? I was confined to a time-out room. Can you imagine telling someone that you don't belong in their institution and then being punished? Distraught, I began to realize that honesty is irrelevant to survival in our world. There was one thing about school that I found at least acceptable; there were times when we were allowed to paint. It was glorious to spatter tempera about and smear my fingers on the paper. I even loved the taste of the paint.

But it had been so different in the world of shadows. To exist there, you needed only to love yourself and your creativity. It brought me joy to see their performances, but it saddened me that I was incapable of joining them. I made furious attempts to vanish like them, and stride across walls in bounding steps. In time, it became clear that I could not. I was rooted firmly to the earth, bound by invisible ropes to the tall, rigid structures of concrete that had been made by people. I loathed my own inability to be a shadow and was left distraught each time I failed. Yet the shadows were patient. They understood that I was unlike them—they whispered reassuring words. I realized they were telling me I was a unique being, that there was no other quite like me. Whether I could emulate them was not important, the shadows were saying. I should be concerned only with things that I could offer, and the areas in which I could grow, not how terrible my failure was. Yes, I understood and I was grateful to the shadows for having shown that to me, because it meant that my real being was what the shadows wanted and accepted. I loved my friends for this, this precious gift of incomparable value.

Why was it that only the shadows had shared that wisdom with me? If humans understood it, then why did they neglect to pass it on to their brothers and sisters? How much simpler life would be if people were accepting of themselves! Then they could actually take time to admire themselves and other people, unburdened by hatred and ill will. I realized that I had a duty to share this beautiful knowledge with the human world, since it was apparent that they knew nothing of it. I told the shadows of what I would do. I smiled and laughed, thinking of the joy that would very soon inundate the lives of humans. I clapped my hands and danced with glee, inviting the shadows to follow my step. And they did, but seemingly with reluctance, their dark faces turned downwards. There was little happiness in their dance, though they encouraged me to go on and do what I felt was right.

I was standing in front of the mirror looking at myself, and I saw a sufferer, someone who had been living off of pain and agony. My eyes were endless hollows—caverns with scars running down their length, and at their end, a wall of bone which was the back of my skull, bits of bone even now being chipped away slowly, and being swept up like dust. Perhaps those bits of bone had been my thoughts, all these fears, things I had believed in, had cared about. My image stared at me and began to decay. I had been living in the husk of a once-beautiful world, I had been inhaling miasma and coughing out my strength. But something else—I realized that I was molting, sloughing off an ugly skin. My dead hide lay on the ground and I was left there standing naked. I gleamed and shone like the sun, like a golden winged insect displaying his colors. I understood then. Yes, I said, this is me. I was earnest, and I went out into the world.

I was quite determined to help the humans, showing them to appreciate what lay within them. If all went as well as it could, everyone would be like the shadows—free and loving spirits, not bound by anything solid or material. So I set forth, a young boy who intended to change lives with my loving gift. I began with the people closest to me—my parents and other relatives, then my teachers and classmates, then strangers that passed me by. Hardly able to contain myself, I blurted out my wisdom and lifted my hands to the sky, overwhelmed with joy. But how my happiness diminished when I was rebuked! People took what I was doing for a childish game. They frowned, scowled and grimaced at me—or paid no attention. I would run through public places crying out in a desperate attempt to pass on my knowledge to someone. Sometimes I would see what I thought was a flicker of understanding in a person's eyes, and then clinging to their pants or dress, I would beseech the person to listen to me. I struggled to make people see that my impetus was love, not

56

frivolity or a desire to play games, but no one wanted to understand. Still I pushed onward, and my perseverance was a source of much concern to parents—they too were blind to my cause and thought I had been somehow disturbed psychologically. This upset me deeply. Couldn't they ever try to see what I was doing?

One day as we were walking down the sidewalk, I saw a man ahead of us walking very slowly, bent over. I knew that this man was much older than me—what everyone called an old man. I could feel the emotions that ran through his mind and body as if they were my own, and what I felt more than anything was pain. A great ocean swept over me, and I nearly cried out. Was this what being an old man meant? As I neared him, I could see that the old man's face was deeply wrinkled, and also deeply scarred. The vestige of some terrible wound cut a ravine across his chin and cheek and eye, and part of his lip, which made it cleft and ugly. Yet I saw clearly that this was a beautiful being, who needed only to love himself in order to bring those things forth to the world. A rushing noise filled my ears, and my heart palpitated. I walked up to the old man and stared into his eyes, which were like vast pools where I could see myself reflected. I said nothing, but smiled with all of my might, and felt myself radiating the light in my heart, all the while looking at the man. He stopped short and looked down at me. The world seemed to hold still for that moment as we looked at each other. Then, the old man opened his scarred lips and croaked, "Don't you laugh at me, boy. Don't you laugh at me or I'll hit you."

Not understanding what he meant, I tried harder to share my gift with him, but then he lifted up his hand over me, and my smile broke. "I mean it. I will hit you, boy. Don't you laugh at me." He thought I had been making fun of him, that my smile had been one of cruelty. In my shock, I was unable to explain to him that it was not so, before my parents had rushed up and taken me away, scolding and castigating me for something I had not done. I tried in vain to express the truth, but they would hear nothing.

I understood then why the shadows had seemed downcast by my excitement and eagerness to share my gift with the world, as they had shared it with me. All my life, a total of seven years, I had been interacting with beings quick to reject something unknown. No, no, this was terrible! And my naiveté shattered like frail glass, I was forced to realize what sort of a world I lived in. It was much more beautiful to think that I had a place among the shadows, that I was to be the bringer of that message of love.

The shadows behaved like artisans, tricksters and fools of yesteryear, leaping about, painting walls and sidewalks with their dancing figures. They performed like glorious actors for me, composed silent songs, delivered mute speeches, scattered about in a flurry of dark shapes. They became drunk with love of life, stumbling about and cavorting. Fights would break out—they would mourn, then melt away into silence. But lo! They were back, showing me it was all a carefree game, a glimpse at their inner laughter, a wild mockery of the fools that surrounded us and an overflowing happiness in the heart.

Oh, I loved the shadows! How they made me laugh.

1990 Bookstore, Washington, D.C.

1990 With Cielo, Central Park, NYC trip with Mama

Journal Excerpts

December 11, 1990

[Albuquerque, age 15]

I'm sitting in the art room with various people, among them my friend M. I hadn't realized what a truly great person he is. He is ruled by the intensity of his spirit, the way all great artists have been, moved with passion, crushed by defeat, tossed about through life by violent upheavals & earthquakes, suffering, but loving it, tasting every moment & savouring it, clinging to it like a lost child to his mother—a thinker, a feeler, a sensualist, expressionist. He once told me something to do with inspiration—about a Norwegian or Scandinavian goddess—& he went to great lengths, with incredible detail, to describe her, how she would fly down from the heavens with streaming blond hair and winged sandals, and how she would take you in her strong, slender arms, pressing you tightly to her divine breast, & take you far up into the sky. And then he laughed & it was over. But it was beautiful. Anyhow, I needed to write that because M. is a great person. Today when I walked into the art room, he looked at me, rose from his chair, & said in the most warm, good natured way, "Itz, my friend, how good it is to see you! I've missed you," & with that he opened his arms & we embraced. He did it in a half joking way, but the very act was practically forbidden, in this homophobic society that fears embracing among friends. There must have been genuine feeling, otherwise why would he have not cared what everyone else thought?

It is now 6th period. The art room is crowded & noisy, but I find that it doesn't affect my writing. I'm somewhat worried about my performance in this class. I wonder if writing my journal is an acceptable classroom activity to Ms. B. She's not here today . . . but I want to do well in all aspects of school. Tonight will be devoted to catching up in schoolwork.

I miss Gillian. I miss her so much it is painful. I wrote a letter to her but didn't mail it off. I have a sense of urgency about our whole relationship. I'm afraid I'll lose her, & somehow writing letters will at least put it off until I can be with her. But right now I've got school to reckon with, & so as long as I'm here, why not carry myself with honor, & a respect for my situation? Still, my thoughts drift to Gillian. I do believe I love her. I would be willing to do so much for her. How much? The truth is I don't know. Yet the words spill out of my mouth, blast out to the winds & the trees & flowers with joy & glory—I love her! And I miss her horribly. The memories of the few brief moments we spent together tear at me because I long for them. . . . There was this look she'd get when I kissed her—her eyes would sparkle, sort of entranced. I love her so much. Perhaps next summer, perhaps after Christmas if she comes down, I can see her. *I want to be with her!*

Last night I spoke with Papi & he seemed horribly sad, depressed. For him, life has taken on a bitter edge or something. He has lost hope for me. As far as he is concerned, I have psychological problems & should seek counseling. We had dinner— his eyes were watery, the way they are when you are about to cry & they're on the rim of your eyelids, veins reddened & bloodshot—he didn't say much—his lips were dry & cracked & he seemed weary. I couldn't understand it. I mean, why is he so out of it? And then I remembered that I had seen an image similar to this one when I looked in the mirror at myself the other day. My face looked somewhat pale, drawn, dry. I am tired these days.

I had really believed I could survive just by working at different jobs & working at my creative arts, & something would work out. Because I'm lucky—like Longshot, the guy in X-MEN, amazing even in his immaturity, graceful even in his clumsiness— he doesn't trip and crack his jaw on the ground—he smoothly tumbles, lands softly, rolls to his feet. I have fallen—I essentially dropped out of school a few days. & *boy* did I take a fall. My inspiration has vanished like a puff of smoke from a match. Yet I know that I'll roll up & fly again.

December 21, 1990 [Christmas visit to Washington, D.C.]

What an incredible day! At around quarter to 7:00 this morning, Mama awoke & made us some porridge. After a few minutes, we had all awakened to breakfast—it was good. The girls went off to school—Mama and I stayed behind, because today was our day together. Anyhow, we slept some more, then I was writing, Mama was asking me to hurry up because our day was going by. I have been taking great care to clean my face. It seems that the climate has a harmful effect on it—I have been breaking out with pimples. I hate the way they look—they make me feel ugly and unworthy of showing myself to others. What would Gillian think if she saw my face like this?

Mama, upon hearing the way I felt about my current state of appearance, curtly returned my statement that I looked ugly & said I looked "handsome & artistic." It made me feel good.

We took the bus to Metro station, & then a subway to the Archives station. Along the way I told her my recent thoughts regarding the past year. What I never realized is that I was really having a hard time with something . . . what I should have done was accept it and do the best I could to help myself get thru it. Instead I hurt myself because I thought my problems were a direct result of my failure to be a good person.

Mama responded in a casual and detached way, like, "Yeah, it was tough for you, wasn't it, honey?"

Yes, of course it fucking was. Couldn't she see that? Hadn't she been in a situation made 100 times worse because she blamed herself for it foolishly? Yes, she had, she said, but things like her age & all the things she had seen kept her from falling a victim to her own pain. Instead she didn't brood over things, so that she helps herself see past them.

I realized the maturity of her actions & decided I would try her way. I felt much better, much freer, much less miserable. Finally we came to the National Gallery of Art—we went straight to the Garden Café and got Trout-Fillet-something. I got Espresso which I've *never had before!* Then I got a cup of cappuccino, which I've never had before either. We are both artists on the same plane, basically searching for the same thing. We rarely waste time arguing over petty things because there is no need to. We talked about what I'm going to do in the not too distant future & came up with several ideas. . . . She's a bit tired & spaced out from her breast operation [early cancer] & I can tell, but she's doing incredibly well.

Before we left we saw a boxlike structure made out of mirrors with an entranceway about 9 ft high & 4 ft wide. It was a room made out of mirrors . . . a sculpture open to the public, provided people wore little slippers instead of shoes so as not to damage the mirror-floor. We tried it. It was incredible. The mirrors were greenish—reflections were cast in every direction. Each step seemed to be a plummeting pitfall, while I could see myself in the floor as if I were above myself, looking down on me. We left that room in amazement.

We rode the subway back to Dupont & went to Second Story Books. I had about $18 credit there and we got interesting books. There was then only time to order a pizza and buy me a soda at the Dorch [Dorchester Grocery] when Stefan was at the door urging me to get my shit together for the drum jam I told him I wanted to go to, too, to celebrate the sun solstice or whatever, in Takoma Park. A man there had long snowy white hair tied back in a ponytail, a sparse white goatee, & huge glasses that magnified his slanted blue eyes immensely. In his eyes were dancing lights & tales of laughter that were centuries old. Candles were lit, lights turned off, & instruments selected. We drummed of lands where snakes rattled their tongues, slapped animal hides, and hummed.

Now the moon is young & the stars are sweet in the sky beneath which I write this.

December 29, 1990

It was getting extremely chilly in the apartment & I got someone to bleed the radiators, but even after they were giving off heat, it was going to be awhile before they got warm. So I sat in Avignon & drank my coffee, watching people pass by, trying to understand each one, sometimes unsuccessfully. When I finished I took the bus & the subway. It has begun to snow fiercely.

My friend looks like a short woman. In fact she is. She is 17. We came back to the apartment and jammed a little. I watched her carefully when she played guitar. A couple of times I brushed her hands when I was showing her hand positions. Her skin is remarkably warm and soft. I remembered the time last year when she leaned over me at her house, her warm soft thighs pressing against my face ever so softly just for a moment, so softly, gently, & I could feel what it would be like to be with her. Many times yesterday I wanted to put my hands on both sides of her head . . . redefine ecstasy for her. . . . I walked her back to Dupont Circle. Her hair, as fine as silk, was draped over her shoulder & I wanted to touch it. I gave her a hug & said I would call before I left. She said she hoped things would work out between me and Gillian.

January 8, 1991 [Albuquerque]

How many days has it been since I last wrote? I *need* my writing, in the same way that I needed my music. There have been too many times when I was on the verge of madness because I wanted to write but didn't have my notebook or the time. I am feeling a deep, profound shock—it's hurting my soul. I wish the semester were just *over.*

Letter to his mother, November 12, 1991

Dear, dear Mama Mama, mama, mama, mama! Mama of joy and electric laughter!
Mama of beauty and an embrace that could encompass the world! How are you?
How I miss you. I miss our talks and our Friday night bashes. I miss your
hugs and your encouraging words and our jamming sessions. When will we have them
again?

Thank you for your tape letter. I suppose I should go about the business of
describing life these days as I know it. It's nothing easy, so bear with me.
Life, life...hmmmm... when will you ever make sense? You are a wonderful and
frustrating mystery. You are like a restless child that must be tended to day
and night, because left unattended, you run rampant and create havoc. Sometimes
you make me want to shriek and pull out my hair. Sometimes I do shriek and
pull out my hair. No matter. I am young and someday you will make perfect sense
to me (so he says, knowing fully that life never makes complete sense). Oh,
Mama. Life these days is difficult. I suppose it never gets truly easy, but this
is a miserable age. There is so much to be understood, realized, dealt with,
sorted out, turned in, collected, processed, spat out, chewed, digested, excreted,
reflected on, discarded, forgotten, taken into account.... Does this get easier
with time? One of the most difficult things for me to deal with is that once I had
the freedom to percieve the world as black and white, good and bad. When I was
younger my situation permitted me to spend all of my time immersed in my own creat
ive efforts with no regard for the outside world. Now the natural process of time
pushes me further and further out into that strange cruel world that surrounds us.
I'm scared shitless. I don't want to deal with it. I could journey out into the
world if it was purely good, if it embraced me warmly and let no harm come to me,
but the world is violently angry and hateful. I can't deal with it. Perhaps you
know what I'm saying?

I read In Crying's Body again this week. It was beautiful. I realized after
reading it that I get writing from you, Mama. I love you.

Tiko

June 10, 1992

[San Francisco, age 16]

Here, in this secluded peak overlooking valleys and ravines of treacherous, bloodstained stones, I am safe. Unreachable. I watch storms howl outside. I drink hot milk & touch my own pale body, and massage my thin hand when it cramps. A few worries, but they can wait. I sit here watching ideas ferment and slither. It is all very good. I have dark glittering eyes—good ones that won't fail me when hardships come climbing up the rocks of my stronghold to assail me. But what am I trying to say?

Strange days, these. Lots of reading & writing, warm coffee drinking, idea sorting. As ever, the hunger for a lover. Wolfish, vulpine, like Hamsun's book—violent, terse, many-haired, long tongued. Stretches back sorely through the spire to the core, tugs. See a woman—ah, sweet agony, want to touch her hair, lips, look into her eyes. But want no rolling royal clouds, Whitmanlike. Get serious & hardy. All is good, I think.

I like silence. The quiet has a sort of mystic fecundating power to it. Write well, & with that vibrant aura about me, catching the people, scenes, the pageantry whirling by—I wish I were on a car ride right now.

I hear a howling, honking snorting sax—animalistic beauty. Hot lady legs extending like fibers of melody. Now a pungent electric guitar—a pin poking your nerves. Hendrix found a way with sound to ride into people's beings & jar them. Now the sound is tumbling in thrumps & blows, one after the other. New scorching riffs succeed dying ones. He flamed! It was the amplified sound of cell division and synapse activity. Boom, blam, rock & screeching roll! People moan & cry in the act of love.

But I want to say just how deep my pain runs. Always there, running in arteries. Sometimes wake up and feel it, caustic, coursing like acid. I hurt. Deer pierced through the neck by a lead slug—not pierced but shattered. I want—no, yearn—yearn for

beauty. Like the white preternatural stag bathed in springs un-
touched by the squalor of the outside world.

June 17, 1992

I have a matrix of unfinished beginnings heaving under my feet. I
have begun on sharp dangerous ground, and without resolve. I am
angry. I feel incapable of finishing what I set out to do. I am also
angered to discover that I have a perception of life that is too
romantic & cinematic. When the going gets rough, I find myself
wanting to quit, to not exist in my situation. I wait to fly off into
the sunset. This is not too wonderful a fantasy to be living in.

If I have a place in the world, it seems to me to be at the fringes, at the border of the cosmos. I feel most at ease when I am not quite functioning within the universe, when I am watching, not included, not recognized.

My situation was high school. I left high school early. I am trying to prepare myself for a career as a writer, If I must be a journalist, a sorry hack, so be it; but first I must know how to speak continuously, beginning, continuing, finally ending having said something substantial and organized.

I stopped writing my book, story or whatever it might be not long ago. Thought has a way of dominating life for me. When writing reaches difficult points, the temptation to think like a maniac and not write a word tends to win me over.

I am terribly lonely. I have never made love with a girl or a woman. . . .

I am just realizing how profoundly important music is in my life. Music essentially enables me to either transform a feeling, to transfigure it for the better, or it cripples me and forces me into the throes of an ugly feeling grown uglier. Music of past centuries composed with art and insight will usually strengthen me. Am I really saying I want tradition, or traditional education? Or am I saying that I appreciate outdated, obsolete aesthetics more than those of my culture because I cannot find fault with them? I *really* want to transcend my own ignorance. I wish I had the will to sit down and feverishly learn what I don't already know. . . . I want to be worth my salt. If I make my mark in the world of literature, it will only be because I have bent myself to my task and dedicated my life to the improvement of my voice and knowledge.

Mama is in her room, reading the compilation of character perceptions that I slapped together and now call my writing [*Face Hanging Like a Star*]. I pray that she appreciates it. One of these years, I'll awaken and find an experienced hand at the end of my arm, a trenchant editor hiding in my head. I will craft & polish fine short stories, put out a book of them when I'm 35, 40, maybe 45. I will have something to my name; I will have no worldly belongings to speak of, except for an unimpressive house on the countryside where I will live with my lover, the woman whom I will love, who will love me as strongly, as unequivocally.

My wife and I will make love often. We will drink coffee and drink each other's tongue and know that we are in love. When we argue we will quickly embrace and find ways to bring conflicts to resolution. Perhaps we will have a child.

I have just changed my mind regarding the piece I wrote. Not bad, when you consider that my voice is yet kind of unschooled and rough around the edges:

Compelling and beautiful. García does not belabor his point. He delivers it with flaring gusto, then curtly withdraws. A milestone in the world of underground teenage literature.
                    —The Fantasyland Review

Brilliant, rhapsodic, full of subtle innuendo and courageous raw dramaturgy. Few writers have conceived such visions and depicted them with such burnished lucidity.

                    —New York Spurious Tribune

Dithyrambic, Whitmanesque! García has written sheer jazz!

                    —Himself.

July 28, 1992

I grow like a tenacious vine, an irrepressible weed that snarls & festoons, knotted, impossible to quell—up I whip & crack & tangle, entrammeling the world. I live! To my friends—the talented, the creative, the wise—I bow. To life I bow. To greatness

70

that surpasses me I bow. I bow like a king before his father—I bow like a warrior before the sun. In life, there are flames that would devour us if we do not dance with them.

August 2, 1992

The city tonight was a gorgeous apocalypse of sounds and flashes. Chinatown, a movie there, bustling people, dinner in a Vietnamese restaurant, a walk up Columbus St., Jack Kerouac & Kenneth Rexroth Alleys, City Lights Bookstore—S. (the glasses, the moustache, his charm)—they were all glorious. "Don't worry, friend. Just take it easy. One day you'll find a woman. She'll see you for the great person you are . . ." he said to me.

August 10, 1992

Work really is my handle on reality, the axis on which my inner-most circle turns. It was such a critical step, finding a job. . . .

I'm scared for my own safety. Maybe I've not got what it takes to walk back into high school & succeed. Maybe I'll never get to college. . . .

I've had a hard day. I'm still healing. I'm still gaining in strength. But I have love & joy—those two, like entwined lovers—always with me.

FACE HANGING LIKE A STAR

A NOVELLA

ITZOLIN VALDEMAR GARCÍA

1992, age sixteen

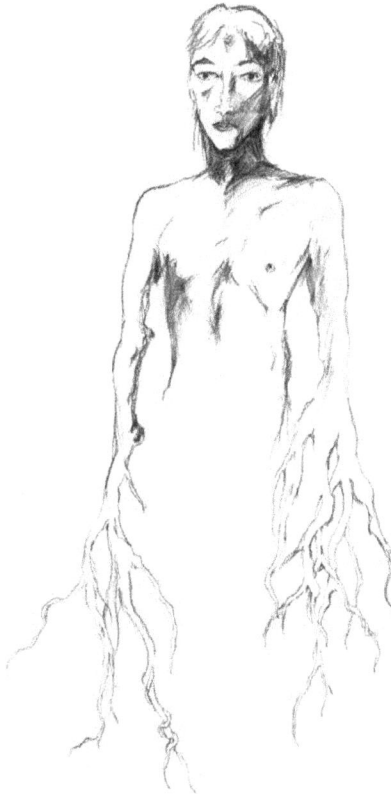

I have the faces of everyone I've ever seen stored in my face.

In Mexico, there are dark places in the midst of the squalor and the pollution where there is no noise, little motion, where one can sit undisturbed. I live in the little village several miles from here. *Here* is El Toro, a bar or café. What could you call it?

The men sitting at the table nearby take no notice of me. They are a world unto themselves. They talk and smoke and drink. Three faces. There is a little light shining down from a bulb on the ceiling. The heat is sweltering. The mosquitoes are sweating.

"What do you say, what do you say? What's happening? It's all sure to collapse. We're not safe here, you know. Three years and they'll pull their switch or whatever it is, we'll all be shadows, incinerated, I'm telling you—"

"Shut up. You think in terms of myths. I want to shatter myths. I'll shatter you if you're not careful—"

"What do you say about my new painting? I swear, I'm becoming fanatical. What do you call it—paranoid. The painting is a zoo. Schizophrenic—"

They talk, interrupting one another, never letting each other finish. Each one feeds off the unfinished thought of the one before him. They are ceaseless.

"My nightmare was good. The lady, she came to me. Her lips were like crabs. She sat nearby, her feet—they started to shoot up in the air. I put down the newspaper and tried to feel her, touch her—her lips, they pinched me, pincers, cutting my mouth—"

"What about the smoke? They say when you smoke a cig-
arette, you should watch the smoke, the way it rolls, and you'll
figure it all out, just like that. I say—"

"Your painting was childish, mysterious. The whole thing was
turning and melting. Like a memory you can hold in your mind,
but it turns and melts, eludes you. You should try lansc—"

A woman opens the door and walks in—the momentary flash
of light leaves an impression on the eyes. I lean my head back and
try to study the image as long as I can—like a Kirlian photo-
graph, but fading. The impression of a woman in a doorway is
archetypal, primal—looking at it there, burned in my vision mo-
mentarily, it seems deeply intimate, one of the first images to
impress itself into the human mind—mother, perhaps—

She sits down at another table and lights a cigarette awk-
wardly. Her features are indistinct, obscure—only her shape is
discernible. She is not old.

"Have you ever wondered, have you ever wondered about
painting as a separate reality? I mean, for instance, what if you
came upon the realization you were creating a living plane—"

"Well, I don't know about *living*. But separate reality, yes.
Look at us now. Focusing our attention—all on the same tan-
gent. It's a new cosmogony, friends, like—"

"Painting atomizes the mind. Look at you two—terrible.
You're already in hell. Say, could you get a hard-on in hell? And
who to do it with? She-devils. I—"

"Time is going too fast. We can't hold onto it. Ever stop to
wonder? We'll never be here right now again. Never. We're not
living enough. We've got to devour the present, or—"

"No, the past is where it's at. Without memories, we're just
ciphers—"

"In my daydreams, it's a different story. The womb is there,
all the time, but it looks like a cameo. The whole thing is too
easy to climb in and out of. I want something warmer—"

There is a dead silence. All three look at the woman. Smoke is
rolling up from their cigarettes. Hers has died. She sits, faceless, a

figure. Her legs are crossed. Her hands are in her lap. She doesn't move. The men twitch; no one speaks.

In Mexico, it is possible to paint alone. Critics and theorizers abound in the city, but the country is left alone. Who would go to the country to paint? It rains much here. The sky is always gravid, heavy, looks like a huge stone hovering over the world. I go into El Toro seldom—when I want to live a waking dream. The rain is good. It gives one the feeling of peace—even during a storm. During the storms, the flowers stand out vividly with unnatural colors. The boys run with their bicycles. The boxes of fruit are left outside of houses. Trees reach higher with their branches to receive the rain. Somewhere next door I can hear ardent lovers embracing, moaning. Such a peace. The world could be shattered in a cataclysm and the lovers would go on making love. Perhaps the girl will conceive today. After each storm, we emerge from our houses, just born—the storm is a kind of universal conceiving, then a gestation, then an emerging—everyone comes out of the houses to look at the world. Mouths are agape, bodies are relaxed. The world is new, flourishing . . .

I paint in here, producing strange, convoluted children. It is so much like a waltz with death—the somber music, the drapery black and enveloping everything. I try to sleep but spend the nights dreaming, and in the morning I remember each dream individually, precisely. I recount each one on the canvas, laboring, sweating. The paintings are black and constructed and sucking, each one like a mass of severed blood vessels clutched in one hand. I am weeping, giving birth, I am dying, I am inseminating.

Reach deeper into the soil of memory—each painting is a billion memories melded only partially, flimsily—each one an image ready to disjoint. I struggle up there, at my summit, at the height of ecstatic painting, hurling myself into the uncharted, finding the work too vague and indistinct—cursing, pacing—back to the work, wrestling with it like I would a beast, gripping hair, horns, *down,* tame the thing. —It throws me forward, where I tumble blindly and feel a loosening, like a child fallen in the street, his coins jarred from his hand—the result of the coin of the soul splotched thickly. I pant, I relax—the struggle does not remit—it pauses briefly.

My spine is being uprooted and injected piecemeal into the painting—the struggle becomes overwhelming, lunatic—the beast is geometric, fractured—I am slipping away on some vast oblique landscape. Disintegration, separation of the whole into its particulate matter. I have been run through by the sun and turned inside out—I am open, the memories are loose.

The air is thick, dark. Breathing is difficult. The darkness is membranous, touching me completely. I do not move, but sit and shudder quietly. The darkness shudders with me now, like a black velvety butterfly fanning its wings, brushing me with them.

When I move, it is to run out into the dirt road outside of my room. I run at first and then walk. The people here clearly do not like me. That is the trouble with dipping the feet into strange waters—a host of unpleasant beings is called up, at once familiarizing itself with you. What do I want with them? The night is cool and free. I walk briskly. The moon is out, cold, gibbous, splashing silver light.

The life by the stream is rich and fascinating—I have given up plumbing the soul's depths for sitting by the stream. To watch. To draw. The grasses and the stones and the trees are cold and moist with dew at dawn. The sun rises slowly and smears their edges with light. One has the illusion at first that all is still. You have only to look closely at the ground to see the swarming life. Here by the stream is an entire miniscule microcosmic order of life—it jitters, it trembles with *élan vital*—and men typically ignore it. They turn their heads and look for a moment, perceiving it as a beautiful motionless scene, something not much different from a painting. Quiescent. How terribly wrong they are!

I usually come here at dawn with paper and pencils and shiver in the early morning cold. I warm with the world in the sunlight. Later on the children come. We are the only ones who enjoy this place. The children—jubilant, like grasshoppers leaping. They come and splash in the water, forgetting themselves, hurling mud at one another. They lift up insects and scrutinize them, kiss the earth, pick flowers and scatter their petals irreverently.

I become a child too. I am too big to run with them, but I lean against a tree and watch. I laugh loudly. The mothers watch me from their houses. Sitting against the tree, turning life over and over in the mind while the run rises—it is such a maze up there in the mind—better to forget it in the company of children and sweat in the sun, watch the dark-skinned kids wrestle in the grass.

Soon their fathers will take them to work, God knows where. They will stop smiling so readily. Hands will callus, arms get scarred, hollows in the face deepen.

I try to draw the flowers and the children's faces. The kids move too quickly. Their teeth are startlingly white—I try to capture this by shading the entire paper with graphite and then erasing, trying to educe teeth from the shadows. The result a blob of smeared gray. I show this to them and they laugh. One boy wants to draw. I happily lend him my tools. He sets to work assiduously, his hair falling over his eyes, he pushing it away now and then with curses. Later he finishes, proudly shows it to me. I laud it, genuinely impressed. I tell him he reminds me of Diego Rivera. He does not know who that man is. The children think that I am strange. They leave me and play.

Already the children are mastering the intricate social system of their parents. The boys exercise brutal dominance—the girls acquiescence. I marvel at the tremendous capacity of children to learn anything they are taught, rapidly, unquestioningly. I want to be a child. I want to shirk my age, laugh and be a grasshopper . . .

The plumbing is repulsive. One can only hold one's nose and pray. The floors, the ceilings . . . a true white man, I consider leaving. To what? The city would drive me mad. But it's getting maddening here. The mothers don't like me near their children. The fathers aren't hostile—they steer clear of me.

Moved into a room—second story—in another town. This one is larger, not as bucolic. Cars pass through. The walls of the house are cracked. Downstairs is a family—father, mother, several children. The woman labors all day, tending to her flock, changing diapers, cooking fiercely. Today it is pork. My belly rumbles. She is such a good wife. Devout. Her husband works all day driving a truck. At night I see him drive up and honk at his children, bellowing orders. Life does not treat them well. The father beats no one—he simply yells. At night, he does not take her by force, but I hear her whimpering fearfully. I am painting again, recalling the image of the woman in the doorway. The whimpers of the woman downstairs give me direction—both women, the one in the doorway and the one downstairs—are faceless, yet they exude pain, an electricity, an inexorable maternal endurance. I try to draw the two women as one, and try to surround them pictorially with the aura that they emit in life. The painting fails.

The heat sickens me. I rot like an overripe fruit. I lie on the mattress most of the day, thinking. I can hear the woman's pot boiling—can smell the foods that she cooks. She toils endlessly. She thinks of nothing but work. Her children wallow or cry miserably. She cares for all of them, yet at the same time she has divided herself into mechanized fragments, a part of her mind for each of the many separate tasks she is responsible for doing. Have

80

a terrible compulsion to rush downstairs and tell her to rest, to take something *back* for once.

At night a sensory dream—the woman cooking, her hands submerged in a cooking pot. Grease everywhere. Explosion of her head into a huge image—her eyes twittering in front of mine. The cilia in her nose not cilia—nerves, extending, as of hands or sensitive prehensile members—her mouth a gory luxurious fruit or florescence—she sings a Mexican mourning song, I can hear her dress ruffled by wind—brilliant flash of light—the negative impression left in the mind—

Leap to paint, knock over the easel and the brushes—my hand smeared over the canvas, paint smudged—disaster. Fuck—I want that image captured, want to lay it down flat, not leave it a wasted mind-image.

Today the shadows in my room horrifically beautiful . . . runny watercolors, India ink bursting and trailing in a pool of water—all of this on the wall. The woman downstairs is pregnant again. Her belly swollen, pushing her dress outwards. Her husband driving away, not returning till late at night, the wife sweating, toiling. Her pot boiling with food. The children screeching. The city outside swelling, growing riotous. The unsafety of leaving the house at night. The grease in the street that the wife pours out at night. Mongrel dogs licking it up. Beggars in the street mutter perversities to her, looking at her silhouette through the screen door. Her baby shifting in the womb, impatient, the gurgling of placental fluid—can hear it, distinctly—lying on the bed in my room, the creaking of the night assailing my ears, infinitesimal sounds exploding against the eardrum——

It is Easter and I am in Mexico City. Manic. Enormous city. Whores and men and children, mothers, musicians, traders, cooks, dancers, prayers—for a minute, I am losing control, unable to register in my mind the presence of so many people, so many shifting bodies, the activity. People do not think here. They move. A beehive. Order in chaos. Terrified, ecstatic, I move, realizing that to stop could be to go under the waves, to be devoured by the crowds.

A huge stone square—a cathedral at its far end. Here there is space to move. Vendors sell fluorescent toys to people, who spin and hurl them. The plaza glitters with fluorescent eyes. Packs of people like thick blots of ink. Huge roaring night gleaming with lights and faces and legs—hurtling Easter eggs. Can hear drums somewhere—deep, not like contemporary drums. Deep Aztecan drums not far away, making the ground faintly tremble. People are approaching. I follow.

In Mexico City there are groups of dancers that struggle to preserve the old rituals of dancing for the purposes of symbolic sacrifice. Such groups teem in Mexico City—at Easter time they take over this plaza and others like it. The people love them— many of them ignorant of the dancers' cause—watching with stone-still wonder as they congregate outside the cathedral, form circles, begin their dancing . . .

They come from all parts of Mexico, many from outside it, each of them led by a chief—some of them more popular, more well-reputed than the others, therefore more respected within the circle of dancers as a whole. They begin coming into the plaza in the morning, but the dancing begins at sunset. They are young men and old men and lost men, all of them caped and costumed, beautiful, wearing plumed headdresses with ostrich feathers and *quetzal* feathers—pheasant, eagle, peacock—costumes adorned with embroidered thread, inlaid stones—standing gorgeous in their groups, each armed with a rattle, some of them wielding shields.

It is completely dark now—that is, the sun has completely sunk—although there is a multitude of lights surrounding the plaza, the dancers light their circle with a flame burning in an earthen pot. The drums pound. They flail their limbs the way the fire flickers in the pot. Their headdresses turn from side to side—the feathers tremble. They sweat. A withered old woman runs about within the circle. She burns *copal* within the fire. The

82

sweet *copal* burns, the faces of the dancers lit by the fire, the night surrounding them glittering multitudinously—they dance, they sacrifice their flesh and blood wholly—the drums pound—the people watch—

Though they pause after each dance, they don't end . . .

At midnight I am still watching. The crowd stirs. A new band of *danzantes* passes through, entering the circle—they are welcomed. The circle begins anew, this time with a preliminary ceremonial dance—*la cruz,* they call it, honoring Catholicism. Then the arduous, frenetic dancing—many of the dancers, old men, gasp as they dance, watery eyes lowered to the ground, legs rising and falling. The young men dance victoriously—they are battling, chests bare, rattles shaking . . .

Later, when the mesmeric whirling of the dancers has entranced us, the audience—as our minds reel in vertigo—the stars spin in the sky—the old woman, *la curandera,* goes to one young man, smears his body with unguent and oils—he goes to the fire-filled urn, slowly lowers his chest to the flames, pauses, then gracefully rises, unfazed. The older men perform a mock sacrifice, leaping over the fire-dancer's recumbent body—they clutch fragments of obsidian—

They leap in the sun dance, Quetzalcoatl's dance, Huitzilopochtli's—then the somber haunting dance of death—one man dressed as Mictlantecuhtli, weaving across the empty circle, his sinuous powerful jerking from side to side, wearing a skull over his face, ancient—

Like a drunk man I finally walk away—catch a glimpse of myself in a store window as I pass—*me parezco como una calavera/*I look like a skeleton—like the pale god of the underworld, or like one of his imprisoned souls—*una calavera,* a skeleton

83

walking his way. Mexico is in a frightful Easter tumult. Even in death, even when Mictlantecuhtli dances, the people rejoice and fling their Easter eggs.

The morning finds me still walking, shivering in the cold of dawn—the sun rises in lurid flames. The city has not yet awakened. The *danzantes* lie in sleeping bags in the plaza. I watch them. I realize how badly I want to be a *danzante,* to sacrifice my useless flesh in praise of *los dioses,* their gods. I chuckle and begin leaving the city . . .

Running and running—with mind if not with body, back to the white simple house, with its cracks, the grease in the street—back to my canvases, my visions. Spiderwebs and shadows thickly woven in my room, the coolness within the adobe walls. Sleeping. In dreams, the lobes of my brain extending until the thought, the feeling, the house rises, disembodied. Huge incorporeal hands of the soul feeling around, curious, examining the room and the surroundings—running along the cracks in the wall, to the freakish paintings, and there I plunge in, touch the world of snarled emotion caged on the canvas—like the men in El Toro suggested—a world created and enclosed within the limited flat space—the painting at first like a calm pearling pool of water—dip in, then abruptly a black recoiling depth—sucked in by the undertow of ululant spirits and my bottled-up fears—all the demons that chase me, that I bury—the sucking constricting darkness of dream-eddy. Crusts of flesh and mass, shaken, swim in this current—in the underworld of imagination—like strange misshapen fish in the fathomless unsounded deep, guided only by neon light glowing at the tip of a protruding member, sucked along like a corpuscle in the pulsing, mauve veins of the subconscious—

The shimmering Kirlian photograph of the woman in the doorway—her electric aureole—her dark shape silhouetted in front of a lightning storm—she is the source—have been trying to paint her for months now, for months striving to swim

84

through the rushing fluid of this womb, burst out, see her stand in that doorway, negative impression, a woman who is a shape cut out of the fabric of life—I the struggling fetus—struggling to cut his umbilical cord and step into that shape standing black and faceless—step through into the anti-matter . . .

W hat could be better than two youngmen walking their way down dusty roads and highways in the late day, laughing with each other and carrying light bags, truant, loud and youthfully obnoxious, absolutely careless? We love a good time, and we're wise as foxes, and tricksters in our own way. Picaros. And we have little in our bags except shirts and journals, where we write our dreams, or stories that we write along our way. The only problem with that is that we're always fighting over who had the idea for the story first. We are good ole boys, someday to be greatwriters, and we have shorthair and strongarms—our stupid brothers have gone off to fight in the war, but not us crafty devils. We are out on the journey of our lives, great, grand, walking the road. We think about greatmen and greatwriters—we think about how we compare to them. We chew grass and swat each other in the head when either of us is unawares. We laugh hysterically and swim in rivers or streams. Waterfalls. Back there somewhere were some hot springs—we saw a couple of naked girls, but they had men with them. Shucks. Another two that escaped us. Chuckle chuckle. Cars roaring by. Someone honks at us. Probably marveling at this fine pair of youngmen roaming the countryside of their motherland. We talk about music every now and then. And Maryjane. Good Maryjane. We laugh. We laugh because our parents did Maryjane in their time, but they've forgotten what it really means, why they did it. Too bad for them. Hemingway now. Why was he great? How really great was he? Girls now. Betty and Melissa back in the city. Betty was better than Melissa. The hell she was. Swatting each other on the head. Fall into the grass on the shoulder of the road. Uncle. Uncle! Walking again. There are great books to be written by greatwriters like us. But for now, we're simply youngmen enjoying life, wasting time, tasting the honey of youth. Sometimes we don't even bother writing. Why should we? There's life to be lived. The next car that passes, we laugh and throw rocks at. Won't you slow down for a couple hungry tired young bucks? Be damned then. We've been walking all day. Looking at the road, and then more road, talking about women and girls and books. And Maryjane. And music. Maybe we should write some before it gets dark? Nah.

Back a ways we met a couple longhairs. Good folks. The gal was nice. Longhairs, hipsters, peace people. Chuckle chuckle. People build fires out here and sit around, talking. Music and love. What a country! We don't have a care in the world, we're all right with everything. Well, why not just throw some flowers in our hair and do some dancing by the side of the road? Everybody loves rock 'n roll. Nothing else at all in the whole world. Should we be greatwriters or rockstars? Both. Hemingway playing an electric guitar. We can do everything, yeehaw, nothing that can't be done by a couple of youngmen walking through their blessed country waving their arms and yahooing in the wee hours of the morning and the afternoon and the dead of night. We'll have a thousand girls each before we're through, we'll write a dozen masterpieces, we'll rock the country and roll the country, then come back here, right here, right to this very point, and lie in the grass and say ain't life beautiful? We might even dance for the people driving by, or sit by the fire with the longhairs. There's nothing can't be done by a couple of young bucks roaming around on the hills. Just grand. Lordy. Let's sit down and write about it.

Now it's time to be greatwriters. We write corny ten-line poems and sit, laughing up a storm in the grass. Ode to the grasses and Maryjane. We clutch our bellies and roll, our faces turning red. A driver stops. We okay? Yes sir, ha ha, fine, ohoho. . . . We've been fine all along. We're all right with every-thing. 'Course, our parents ain't, but that's life. . . . Rolling in the grasses. We'll never get anywhere 'cause we're laughing too much. Get serious. So how much you wanna bet I'll have a girl tonight and you won't? We come up on the road and cross over, and smack the fence with our hands, smiling in summer youngman bliss, and moo like cows, and chew our cud. Yep. American youngmen raising hell, crazy, happy, scaring drivers, dangerous like wolves in a sheep herd. And when night comes, I'm smacking Jim on his back, telling jokes, claiming possession and ownership of that last story. I don't give a damn what he says, I'm the brilliant genius here, not him. Wrestle over it. Uncle! What'd I tell you. It's mine.

Whattyew know, Jim, there's a fire over there, a fire that the longhairs probably built, where they're probably sittin' right now, drinkin' a little and talking and having some fun. And we go. And indeed there're longhairs sitting around a fire. But they ain't drinking. And they ain't loving each other like some others do right there for all to see. They're just sitting there as if someone's died, and they have nothing to say at all. How might you all be doing? They look at us and a couple of them might be smiling, but you just can't tell. Jim and I don't care. We just sit down with them. We're youngmen and soon to be greatwriters. We don't need an invitation. The fire is a good one, huh? Well it is to me. The longhairs are stern and thin, and they look they're in a world of hurt, or they've been through one all their life. They just sit there and appreciate the fire quietlike, and sometimes they lean on each other's shoulders. But they have no Maryjane, and they have no peace songs to sing, and they don't care whether we're there or not. They're sure as hell not going to talk.

Jim doesn't care. He sits there, a strong youngman who doesn't care about jackshit. If they sang songs, he wouldn't care. And he doesn't care that they aren't. The longhairs are thin. Real thin. And the two women sitting with their two men look like they've lost their babies, every last one of them, stillborns. They're probably thinking about the war. I hear people talk about dying babies and such, babies dying over there, getting shot, and maybe that's what's ailing them, these babies over there, and not their own. I don't know. The fire's dying, the longhairs are getting up, leaving. One of them leans back, asking with eyes-only if we're going to follow. Jim doesn't look up. You want to go with, Jim? *Nope*. I do. *Fool, what do you want with them?* I don't know.

Jim's gone. He's hitching back, or maybe farther away. He didn't say where he wants to go. I'm staying.

We walk through the woods together, silent. I don't exactly feel welcome. But they haven't told me to leave. Why not stay? There is little light. I can see the figures of the longhairs vaguely, but I mostly follow with my ears. Jim is gone and I'm here alone with longhairs, and I don't even know what I want. Here we are walking in obscure woods in the middle of the night—to where I don't know. I don't feel like laughing any more about anything. We walk towards another fire up ahead. As we approach, I espy a sort of ramshackle shelter or some such thing. I'm nervous in the pit of my stomach. Now we're in front of the fire and looking at the people gathered in front of it. There's an old woman and old longhaired men, all of them woebegone and wasted and unsmiling. Who are you, one man asks. Just another American I say. Fuck America he says, and takes a drink. The angry distraught longhairs sit by their fire and stay there, and I watch these angry men with teeth missing pass their whisky and mutter now and again, spitting it out. Nothing beautiful here. In a strange way, I want to cry.

After hours, everyone just sort of seems to accept that I'm staying, and they don't say anything cruel to me, and they speak a little more. Mary is the old graying woman, and she seems to own the tent and have a huge battered bleeding heart that she gives to the other longhairs, and she drinks too, and now and then puts her forehead on another's shoulder and cries terribly. Her husband is in jail. I don't know his name. He's a longhair. The other men are fierce and bitter and drinking, passing their bottle, depreciating America, teeth missing, their words whistling through the gaps. They have no love to give to outside people. They have no peace to share, no hands to extend. Fuck America. They look like men in prison, men looking out from prison cells, on whose walls are inscribed vulgarities, where dark interiors reek of piss and misery. Peace? Love? What are you talking . . .

A day and a night. A couple families passed through here during the day. One had a dingy beat up station wagon, from whose back window several white-faced ghostly children looked at me. The family picked up some of the old bitter men. They talk of John, the imprisoned husband, and who cheated him, and who's corrupt, and when they're going to talk to who about bombs. Violence. These people are desperate. They want to use the very things they curse to better their world. They don't give two shits about folk singing or joining hands or eating healthily. They want to tear the government apart and piss on it. But Mary is not so angry. She doesn't want anything except to cry and bleed in her heart over her husband, and hold her many children to her sweaty bleeding breasts, and sit in front of the fire weeping until she is gone and gone more. And in the night, after the day has passed, I follow everyone into her tent where there is a candle burning and eagle feathers hanging, where there are dozens of sacred possessions and items and amulets of wanderers and bleeding drinking longhairs who have lost the ability to laugh over the darkness of the injustice in their country . . .

And in there I get hollow and empty, and I cry, not for myself, but out of the weariness, the desperation that compels these souls, and I sit there in a circle, angry and wrathful and wasted, drinking, and fuck America, and fuck my youngman joy, and where is my strength?

The next day I think about Jim, and where he might be now. In Colorado. Or home in the suburbs and necking with his girlfriend. He is getting letters from his brother and thinking about what a good youngman he is, and wondering when he will be a greatwriter.

Life is a constant oscillation between different emotions and states of being. Capaciousness is a flat circular configuration at birth that begins spinning. The experiences that we undergo, the memories we cultivate—they make impressions on the spinning circle. Perhaps we continue receiving impressions into old age. I know only that in these days my ego constantly slips into indentations in the plastic circle of consciousness—it sleeps in the hollows that were pressed in by some early experiences years ago—in childhood—and thus I feel myself to be a child. Because I am perfused by this new mood, or mode of perception that began in childhood, I view the world with a child's eyes—the scope of my vision narrowed, the breadth of my awareness lessened. In truth, I am innocent. One could ask for nothing more than re-experiencing the world as a child.

The atmosphere is good today. Health. The world is young, vernal. Trees supple and flowers bursting from buds. Wind fresh and blowing. The sailing, wafting—like silk in the zephyr—of young girls' hair. People are shifting almost imperceptibly—like the flowers, they strain against the skin, the bud that encompasses them, that constrains inner growth. It is life in a slow motion movie—even the old ones are taking off their caps and their jackets, sitting on benches in the parks, and bursting forth with this new incandescent flower of the soul. I can't change with them. How can I explain to the world—I am living in a childhood dream. I have no blossom. But they don't listen, indeed, they couldn't care less about the flower, out of the many, that isn't swelling irresistibly, dying to bloom in the spring rain.

But I love it—the whole thing. The world is iridescent, it wants to grow new grasses and flamboyant weeds and words. If the old ones can throw away their glasses and shabby coats and dive into the miracle, why shouldn't I?

Closing my eyes—the past is a molten gold trail ribboning away into crepuscular infinity, I want desperately to go back and touch it. Memories, giving me their faint scarce breath, like after a tryst in the woods, still tasting and feeling a lover's breath and lips, watching as she bounds away asking me not to forget her—how could I?

The times are wretched, deplorable. . . . A war against reason. Though shoved into a corner of the world and ordered to stay, out comes surrealism with spider legs, treacherously gleeful, and the sane ones finally begin to understand what's been hiding all this time. Napkins and hankies are produced, tears shed. The point is, it wasn't poison they were shunning—it was life. They still don't understand. Neither do I.

"The Sanctuary" they call it—haven for artists, for the down and out, for the free-minded and the weary. The owner an eccentric woman with a fat purse who wants to save all impecunious bohemians, or at least give them a bowl of soup and a place to

stay. Most of them are beyond hope of reform, but they leech wonderfully, and have the owner convinced she's some kind of demi-god. They all paint her in the evenings.

In this place I have a room—small, dark, tightly enclosed, and I again find myself sealed in with the shadows, forced to look inwardly, to examine myself, to see what, over time I have become, why I became this—forced to watch myself falling into the unique separate indentations in the circle of consciousness, rising from them, empty for a time of emotion or identity, falling again into some new indentation impressed in childhood where consciousness becomes enveloped in the mood of that pocket of memory. . . . It is an endless cycle, one that will only continue to expand and attain higher levels of growth, an indefinite rotation of the soul and the age, and the melting, mutable music that accompanies it.

My Mexican blanket is in the small room—there I repose and think, changing. Every hour on the hour it is a new life. Chameleon. I change wholly and entirely into a new character. A new persona summoned, adopted, absorbed. Then cast aside. I begin anew, afresh, hungry for the image that has not yet been lived. I could go on like this for centuries, devouring new lives, consuming these moods that I fall into. Like a rapid *samsara*.

When I leave the room, I walk down a hallway in the Sanctuary that leads to the main room. Paintings and mirrors on the walls and millions of reflected images and rays of light. To see one's self there, in the mirrors, to touch the enigmatic stuff of the being, reach in, palm it, spreading apart the curtains of consciousness, Slithering in the labyrinthine core of the ego. And walk away, dumbfounded. I leave understanding less than when I came.

In the main room, they are always painting the proprietress. She sits on a chair like a great bird, her face chiseled and thin and altogether haggard, like a long block of stone worked over by a blind master. She loves us, she says. Her clothes are red and foppish—her wealth so apparent as to make one recoil. Kali, I call her. When she looks at the drained, grizzled men that wander into her warm sanatorium, her eyes widen and goggle, deep shimmering gems. I wonder how safe she is, how really and truly generous she is sitting there on her chair transfixing jaded worn men in her house who couldn't fight for their lives, too weary . . . like a female mantis in the mating ritual.

The sun shining through the window rolls carpets of light over surfaces. The time ticks by with terrible slowness. I do not like it here—this woman, or her get-up, or her grey empty sanctum. I go back for my Mexican blanket, through the shattered reality of the mirrored hallway, and walk out. But the world outside, too, has false frightening undertones. My steps are not my own, the surroundings too vacant. Vague suspicion that if I leaped forth I would tear through a movie screen and find an audience watching me on the other side. But I walk.

Can see, up ahead, in front of the reddening evening sky, a friend who I met in the Sanctuary. He greets me. We go for a ride in his car. His vehicle is dark and musty. I tell him so. Like an old carriage, I say, full of mud brought in by passengers who have been strolling in the rain. He laughs. *Rather excessive,* he says, my description. But the world—it has grown huge and has a mighty upward thrust—stretching far up into the vault of heaven like a gothic chapel. It shimmers and glows with amber beauty. Why, isn't that peculiar, I mean, the world, it's gotten almost Byzantine out there—this I say to him—and one could almost expect to see buttresses and bricks. *No my friend*—this he says—*that imagination of yours, getting you into trouble. Don't take these ideas too seriously, one mustn't do that, else we'll go mad.* Yes, I must agree. You're quite right. *Have you ever owned a cat,* he asks. No. Certainly not. *Pity,* he says, *they're remarkable,* and his daughter has one she named Tom, a lovely little calico. That's funny, I say. Why would you name a female cat Tom—I mean, I thought calicos were always females—aren't they?

93

My friend vouchsafes no answer. He is a fine man, I think. He sits in front of the wheel, carrying himself like the captain of a ship—but he is too silent. And every now and then he looks over at me sardonically, uttering nothing, but saying with his eyes— *No, my friend, you are wrong.* His demeanor chuckles at me. His daughter's calico cat chuckles at me. The Byzantine empire whirling past the window—it too, I think, finds me amusing. Good. My friend thinks me a funny fellow.

All at once, he has glasses. He is scholarly, deeply read, aloof. *The Mausoleum of Sultan Hassan,* he says. Hmmmm? *Ever seen it, my friend?* Why, no, I haven't. *Pity. And I thought you a learned fellow. Would you like to get out now? I could let you out at this street, if you like.* Outside a ruddy stupendous world of mosques and spires gleaming, the faint sound of seraphim singing. *Would you like to get out now*—he asks it again. No thank you, friend. I'd like to keep riding. I don't ride much in cars. But, really, where are we going—won't you tell me? *Oh, nowhere* (laughing at me). *You don't get out much, do you?* No, if I am truthful, I don't get out much. But look here, if I am going to be truthful, you're being quite agitating—can't you see what a state of quiet I'm in? And where on earth did you come from—you don't feel real to me, and I'm very nearly trembling with apprehension right now, and you don't seem to be reacting

in any way other than with that confounded laughter of yours—are you listening to me at all? No, I have never seen any sultan's mausoleum, or any Turkish bath, nor have I ever heard of a lady calico named Tom—and why are you driving a car, you a penniless artist who is taking refuge with that terrible woman back there?

We are driving. Schoolgirls are filing out of some new sultan's mausoleum. My friend is quiet. He laughs at me every now and then. I can't understand. Of course, it's my friend confusing me—I'm well aware of that. He seems very familiar to me now. Perhaps we fought together against the French, I ask. No my friend. Impossible. I don't care what he says. The man is quite mad. And he doesn't understand. None of these poor souls back there can apprehend the tragedy that they are living—their queen, their Kali is trapping them all—they are fertilizing her and soon she will clean them up nicely. For her, life is a game of procreation and beheading her male servants. Oh, but Byzantium is a glorious place to be right now. I laugh with my friend. We are riding in his car and laughing together, laughing at the mausoleums and vaults, at schoolgirls, at the calico cats, at Kali and her house. I clap him on the shoulder. *You're quite a fellow, my friend.* No you are, old boy. Hah hah. *Byzantium. Precious.*

Just outside the city, he lets me out, and I sling my bag over my shoulder, remembering the war, thinking of what my home will be like when I return. And I must show my sketches to my brother. He will like them. Funny place this world. What war have I really fought? I try to signal to my friend and call him back, but I'm stuck. Afraid. What has really happened? Night is coming on. Now I am remembering Kirchner—his tortured maddening self portraits—hands missing, the colors. He certainly fought in the war.

At school I am the only ugly thin girl—all the others are the well-fed and big-breasted daughters of bankers and businessmen, and they laugh in a mocking way when they gather, as if to tell me that I will never have their lovely sensuous voices, or their blonde tresses of hair. I try not to care, but my shoulder blades poke out freakishly when I walk—my breasts little bumps that scarcely disturb the smoothness of my grey and only shirt stretched out over my thin body. I am ugly and I know it—and they know that I know it, and when I walk, they laugh a bit, but take no real notice of me, and I scowl and spit as my uncle would have done. I curse to the best of my ability—I struggle to utter the most sordid obscenities at the grey sky and the pigeons and the statue of Saint Ann floating on her wings at the threshold of the school. I try to be the filthiest incarnation of ugly thin femininity that I can, so that they will laugh and abhor me, so that I can bite my lips firmly and make them bleed, and know how terrible I am, and know that I have reason to hate every one of them.

Like a grey wraith with black eyes and red bumps for breasts, my lips thin and purple, wearing pants that do not fit me, my grey shirt, carrying my bag—in this way I move through the school and watch the grey movie that takes place around me. When questioned, I stutter and then straighten my face, trying to be calm. I answer again, this time more coherently and intelligibly. Sometimes I can make perfect sentences, but other times, halfway through the sentence, I begin stuttering again, my eyes fall low, and I can no longer speak. Oftentimes I trip while walking. I am like a bird with legs that wobble under it, too long for graceful action.

Today I do not care. I enjoy the attenuated angular frame of my body. I enjoy the tiny protrusions of my breasts. I enjoy my long black knotted hair falling about me like yarn. I whisper through my purple lips all of the English words that seem beautiful to me, delighting at the timbre of my own voice as it utters foreign sounds. I am friends with a girl named Sara who has acquired an affection for me. She calls me her sister and we embrace after school, running along together. Yet I am still not like her and I know it. She is majestic, even in moments of error or crisis. She brushes her hair back and smiles and speaks like a goddess. I love her. She thinks of me only as a curious being—I strike her fancy, nothing more. She does not think I could understand her heart, therefore she does not open it to me. At times I want to open my creaky throat and sing for her, so that she might smile and say to me, "Now I see. You are beautiful. I was wrong to hide my soul from you." Nothing of the sort happens. I am far too embarrassed to sing, and I know that my song would be hideous anyhow.

I am learning to write. Today I write a letter to Sara in which I tell her that I love her more than life itself, and that I am her subservient companion always. I never give it to her. She would laugh. Today she kicks her legs like a mare and throws her hair out like a queen and dances with joy because she and her friends will be doing something. I glower enviously from my chair and grip the desk until my hands are pale, and then I look away. I do not care for her. She loves nothing in life except herself.

The school is something out of my nightmares. It is mighty and far-reaching and it throws itself up into the sky with sharp points. Its walls are covered with green moss and vines. I look at the entire thing as I walk through it, wondering what it might have to say if it could speak. Perhaps it has seen another dark lanky Israeli girl like me in its long sullen life. I hate this monstrous school and its blonde chuckling students. I hate the lovely princesses and their spinning embraces in front of the school in the mornings. I hate the reflection of my body when I see it as I pass by windows. My voice is the most terrible thing of all—when I speak, it comes forth broken and faltering. I want more than anything else to be beautiful.

I love a boy now who stands every day like a commandeering captain against the wall and says nothing but takes in everything with reddened tired eyes. He is growing a beard already and his hair is thick and bursts and twitches in the wind, and I want to reach over and touch him, or his hair, and say, "You give me strength, and when I see you I sigh with love and feel like perhaps I too am beautiful, or maybe not, but at least there exists some kind of beauty beyond the blonde joy of this school, and—"

But I can't do this either, and he simply stands and watches, a detached poet captain who maneuvers the savage beat of life through the rough seas and doesn't say a word to me or anyone else, and I love him so, and want to give my thin dark body to him, but can't because he wouldn't love it. I am a twisting sliver of rotten wood, driftwood, and I have been thrown up onto a shore that is too beautiful for me. The sea has vomited me up, and now I can't find my place.

I have learned a few more English curse words and now recite them every day with gusto. My breasts are tender and raw and swelling like rosebuds that need to flower—at night I am dreaming and I can feel my breasts growing, and the wind is touching them like a friend and I curl up in black fetal ugliness, longing for some huge metamorphosis into a flashing dark beauty. I look down in the dream to find little wiry fiendish hands pinching my nipples—my breasts grow and swell painfully, and I lift my ragged-haired head and ask myself if this is what it means to be a dark woman on this earth. I cry softly. I wake up thinking of Sara and wondering if she is still my friend. I have no friends. I am an absent invisible entity. In the corners where I take refuge after the day has passed, I grow sparks in my belly and feel as though I house some dark ugly child that will grow up and fight the world and introduce his potent curse language to all, making them see how painful it is to grow ugly and twisting and thin like a vine or a desert-plant, warped by the sun. I imagine that I throw the ropes of my hair around all of the people and reel them into my embrace. I squeeze them unkindly and cry in their faces and sing spiteful songs in Hebrew into their shocked eyes. And to Sara I offer a brooding song about death and the parting of loved ones.

My face is riddled with blackheads. I grow pubic hair. My bones stand out more sharply than ever. I think I am beginning to look more beautiful. I am wearing better clothes and speaking English like one who has spoken it from birth. It feels good to seem American and look around and say, "I don't give a fuck." I try this often. Quickly, rapidly I am entering a new stage of development. I leave the Catholic school and go into a high school. Here there are lots of people. They don't treat me as an outsider. I do not retreat passionately to corners any more. I walk and swing my hips. I am beautiful. I watch men look at me as I pass

and I know what they think. I am aware of the entire world. I have power. I could give birth to a child and I could take a man for myself, if that were my desire. I can go on walks and have my own thoughts. And I can write these thoughts, and I can mutter, "I don't give a fuck" whenever the ignominy of being a dark woman becomes intolerable. I like to take walks when the wind blows because it throws my hair back and I feel cool and free, and life trickles into my hands and feet, jangling, burning. And I feel my own beauty and forget shame, and learn to carry my shoulders proudly, so that their angles are high, not slanted downward, as they were before.

I have friends. They are not like Sara, but they are more like me. They quietly sit and think, and they ask my questions about life, and we share experiences. I see my own worth now. I grow infuriated when someone tries to step on me. I yell and snarl—I point my finger and declare my anger, and clearly state what has happened that is wrong, and if the person does nothing to apologize, then I attack them with words, and assail them with the darkness in the pit of my stomach, and show them what sort of person I am. "I am me and I am proud," I shout.

I am living in the center of the cold city, and I am attending the university. I study constantly. My courses are difficult, but when I pass them, I will feel even stronger than I do now. I have work at a café in the downtown area—I am simply the cashier there. I enjoy the place. The poets, the hippies, the unconventional frequent it—candles are always burning, and incense—tie-dyes spread out on the wall in great curtains. My friend Serena comes in often to greet me or talk during my break. I don't like to talk with her much—we always seem to discuss pointless topics—but she has many boyfriends, and when she brings one of them in with her, I find that I can sway the conversation to greater points of interest. One of her lovers plays the guitar and writes songs. He is taciturn and withdrawn, but when he sings before an audience, his sharp poignant voice makes the blood boil. He sings about societal unrest, the political crises of the country. I listen to him whenever I can.

Months pass. I strive to learn something on the guitar. It is a difficult instrument—my fingers tremble uncertainly in my first attempts. I grow blisters, then calluses. I can find no one who is willing to teach me, so I go to folk music festivals and watch the performers carefully. After their shows, the musicians are often willing to play with people who stay nearby. I leap up into such opportunities, frowning with sincerity. People laugh at me gently, asking why I want to play, or how I can hope to play with such delicate hands. I grow indignant. I wring knowledge about the guitar from my surroundings and drink it, and when I think I am learning something, I work harder. Finally, I am a fairly good guitarist. And I learn to sing with my once ugly voice. And I sing for those around me. And I let my hair grow long down my back, and I let my name be known to everyone. And I write many songs about my experiences, and I look directly into the eyes of the young and old poets and radicals and hippies that come to the performances. And now and then I say, before I begin singing— "Anyone here who ain't with it?—Well, I don't give a fuck."

I find an old smiling Indian with his guitar and his cap who wants to play with me. "Well what have you got to offer?" I ask. "I got good music," he says. "So show me," I say. Right there he throws open his case and his fifty some years of life spill out of his old rude instrument, and I cry, and join in with my voice on the fourth verse. "You can play with me any time," I say. So we do a gig together at the café where I used to work, and we make people laugh and sing, and when it's all over, when we've made a scant bit of money and we're tired, he says, "We'll never be famous, but we're damn good." "Yeah," I say. He goes off, waving. People are talking and smoking joints outside my apartment. I smile and pass through them, going upstairs into my little room, where I sing myself a song and burn away all the pain of youth with calm tears.

*B*ut, be real—*you have no other place. That's a fact. So it is.* She is my aunt or my sister and in a subtle way she parents me—I suppose I should feel grateful, but instead I am almost bitter as if she could be doing better. Fuck the saxophone-screaming, depreciating metal, scraped with paint and fingernail washings. The honk and crashing glass of the city life, the grey cloud moth, and whining of moaning drones. She was a little obtuse angel sitting quietly and pouring out manuscripts of sweetness— What do you think—I mean really—is it good? Corrections? And, my sweetness, could you say more, so that I can come out whole and shining—jigging my neck and so loose winsome like the dancers or *houris* you always talk about—

Yes well, you've got hair like silk and I'd like to dreamlike reach over and kiss you darling (daaahrling) but you wear sunglasses like a masquerade or menacing glasses and I can't compete, and I'm frightened of your hot air and upwards-rising temperament and richness and outpouring wealth. New York, you say, but do you mean it, and when was the last time you took off your silk and bathed unclothed in the sun and sweated for purity's sake, you're—yes, pristine—but also perfumed and stuck in that world of eyeshadow and such creamy cosmetic etcetera.

I didn't like the dark swarthy messiah screaming in the streets that he hated the rich white America—and by god that's what she is, my aunt or sister, rich white perfumed houri dancing and her angelly manuscripts, aloof puffy and heavenly up in the clouds and from the vantage point of clouds and silk and cream looking at reality and not quite seeing, but believing it is seeing—wearing earrings expensive and so opulent, yet they look like candy or plastic. Heh.

The cars are enormous and buses trampling me and the green filthy river of street grunge filling gutter cracks and shoes, everyone filing through, pushing into the dingy crap crack.

It is life all over again here. Nothing quiet or sure, although I am grateful to my sister for such largesse. Quiet and nothing but sit and drink coffee with fifteen-syllable names.

I really wish I could find a quiet and empty-of-civilization-type place to work. People so obtrusive these days and space and time so needed. What do you think?

She was really frightening now, sitting poised and model-perfect—the backdrop of Hollywood glamour and sensuous whispering coolness and the whole hokey act of well honey I got mine and don't you love my lips and tits.

"Well yes, I suppose more cushions needed and expensive luxurious pillows and tea now or coffee later" and would you like my shoes and my nylonned loins are all the way up in the magazines and the vogue is mine, all mine, and—

I am little twisting Dostoevski figure with Egon Schiele colors and little rouged crying cheeks, but she rather didn't care and went right on pompous and high-blown-lipped of the upper class—will she ever notice how filthy, how unpolished her little cherub and brother is? I mean, what the fuck does she see in a little gum wrapper flung away with the flick of the genteel wrist

of a man, and what why, what needs must be done to keep getting her to love me, me.

I'd found a little stone place, its walls angular and gothic—along with gathered entwined-in-conversation people, who sat and drank, booted and beautiful with the gem earrings. And the highblown wonderland talk and their fun amused me, and I sat in quiet, undisturbed—and asked why in the world and boy yeah was it a wonder—my sister will love me now, the genteelness of it all. I couldn't really buy into it, but the patterns of thought were warm—semi-trance of talking and whispering, and reaching under the table to give a non-verbal message or indication of warmth—

A little bent brown man played his warped gypsy guitar in the courtyard whilst it was all Italian Mediterranean and the Spanish shutters on the doorway, and the salty wind, and the huge courtyard with benches and lavender flowers, the couples and the cupids outcropping and outgrowing from the fountains—ahh it was a wonder to take in, not the least of which was the little Saracen girl sitting with boots and a scarf and eyeing the world with purple-hued eyelids and little vibrant red lips, and the entire concrete empty yet living place, and the dream and vacancy and exploding wonder of it——

Where did I want to go? I wanted to be that young penniless chap over there with his hat and humble downward-drawn eyes and the whole quiet-young-sheepherder effect, playing in the moment, and I wanted to lure in some great mystery or occasion in which I would reel, and the purple sky high blooming, heavenward-lifting—upwards stream, upwards—could I be a modest rustic sheepherder if my sister in her tinkling perfumed jewels asked me to, or if the angry stamping beggar stopped declaiming and stomping and the monster of the city buses and cars and—

And a lucky teenage gigolo, who had struck luck with a big grand sleek dame of rich-woman position, they were riding in a car and he smoked slick and quick, you knew his ennui was just an act, inside he was leaping and popping like so much happy popcorn—"Wow, a rich bitch and her satin bedroom, and here I am, whoa."

To New York, and New York again, and doubled intensity because of all the persistent ugly scrambling-for-a-buck types that fill the avenues, and a dirty stream of along-the-way steamy and seamy joints, like parlors of a certain type, and the characters there, smoking-in-leather types, and pollution of a buzzing place filled with pollution all over again, the works—

New York, as viewed through the left window and the generous open space of the square glass image—and the loveliness of a busy city, like looking at the cross-section of a bee hive or ant nest split down the middle with a sheet of glass—and the river of colors, and New York a screaming rainbow ice-cream cone turned upside down and mashed onto the running cars and angry people—streaming sugar all through the streets. The skyscrapers upward phalluses or big hitchhiker thumbs. From above I look, and motionless sit and watch, cradling my own shoulders, as in a solemn Munch drawing, the shadows and the space palpable and unwelcomed friends, and sit on the chair childlike and watch and daydream.

The loft, or studio. Cold. Shivering and unprotected. I am thin and beautiful and that is why Marie likes me, and that is why

I sit here nude and shivering and like a lamb bathed in sun juices and sweet grass and waiting for mother lamb. I am her treat or pet or artist-in-residence. The swarming angry ones down there would kill me for living this way. The thinness and kindness of self-entwined waiting and watching the city, uncaring, watching the hideously warped and refracted image of the real world through the window, staring, a kid observing through a car window the revolutionary unrest of his world and not caring, and oh wow what should I do, nothing I guess, go on watching—the thick sound of noiselessness and I like the feel of my heart and my veins. I want to read and explore and redefine the thick material of internal aesthetics and window-watching and overturned ice cream sugar. The uncivilized windowtop speculation and revolutionary spinning from maddened dizzy tops of lofts and buildings, and waiting for Marie and her psychoanalysis of my distorted artist's mind—and her notions about genius and neurosis and possible connections between the two—and waiting for Marie and her hello and warm embrace and hello honey how was your working at the creative pursuit day? Huh, how did it go, and are you happy to see me, and will we make love or will we discuss new propounded theories about upturning Sumerian vaults and the fractured symmetry of neo-Cubist bullshit art—or will we coil about each other like primal snakes of wrath and energy, coiling and strangling each other's life throb essence, and time choking, and the dark seepage of the soul turning and tumbling in the cosmic vacuum continuous—almighty yoni of goddess let me kiss thy womb and the loin—the curvature of spinal mothers caring and old wrinkled charm tweaked out of a smile of aging people holding each other before conventional fires of the hearth, and then tomorrow clean off the stains from the sheets, because we don't want to leave that kind of evidence, but for now look earnestly into one another's eyes and say clearly and devoutly how much we truly are in love, and the glory of dreaming together on vast dream treks on cloud substance and arm in arm, and waking up in the morning smiling aloud?

And the sheepishness of realizing how sexually magnetized toward each other like opposite poles on the magnet, and now let's talk about my painting, love, after we've made love, and I'll show you these vast new conjured-up archetypes, from the well of being, that sit there, etched or imprinted and ineradicable—the drawback to painting, inasmuch as what you've now already set down can't go, has got to stay—like the vulva images that permeate the fabric of unconsciousness after love, the brief flashing bits that surface and rise like bubbles through already-cut apertures and lose themselves in the riot of time and thought, and don't you see, don't you see baby that this is love, and it's not even about my painting or your office work, but about this synthesis of the womb and the lingam, and this juncture at the apex of your legs or stilts and the sculptural beauty and effusive gasps of verbal African rhythms to the drum of heartbeat echoing the salvaging cooing and bleating of us in that primordial first dance out on the pubescent plane, where we are locked in sunny sweaty embrace, and the portals through which we emanate as though we were never really apart, but sleeping together through one long morning whose evening never came, and now we wake on this grassy plane in a redolent nest, our thighs pressed, desire imprinted in the innermost coils and gusts charging together and slam, the fusion, the completeness of union, coition, and the art and painting and work is done there, baby, not here or outside or yesterday, but here in this locked fused tree of amalgamating love bites and neck kissing and the sweeping currents of hair over eyelids and softly tremulous encounters and reunions of cheeks and lips and all the sweet softness of royal England and such high-browed people, all young and naïve, who tried to be supercilious, but when the dice were rolled couldn't help gasping and falling into each other's swaying

106

arms like Werther wanted to so much and there gasping and saying love, I've begun, or been born, and renascent arts of love and divine conjugation—

And that is love, my sweet love with a soft neck and cubist lovely long-like-one-of-Modigliani's-women girl—you are the one and when you stand momentarily and briefly in the doorway, our hair sings and looks like sunrays sweating from the rooftop, I can't help stirring from the bottom of my being to reach forth and meet that present reality of your hair and charm and self, like dark potent reality and I love, how to put, the embrace and the landlocked crushing sweetness of interlaced soul——

Marie loves me, I think. She says nothing of the sort, it's just the way she caresses me in the morning from beneath the sheets and I whirl internally like a pool of water cleansed by a typhoon—aaaah, who am I, good—and she appreciates too the kindness of such affectionate gestures as kisses or the quick touch on the back of the shoulder just before she lifts herself from the bed. We are truly in love, the veritable factualness of a delicious harmony and how can I even explain such hormonal and biological facts—it's the touch, the kiss, the breath. . . .

But Marie what really do you want from me as your lover and silly artist-in-residence, and why do you sit around ignoring the fact that I am a kind bum and nothing more, and don't even work except to make an occasional image on a three-year-old canvas that should have been finished long ago—what should I do, baby, dearest, my sweetheart?

Baby you just don't understand that I love you and the things that you do, and if that is too much to accept, then you just can't recognize the significance of tongues kissing in the mornings or wet fingers loving in the bathroom while I bathe and the slow music plays, and nothing moves except subtle beautiful bodies in the shakti dance and rhythm—baby, don't think about it, after all you're an artist and thoughtful and way too introspective, and you just shouldn't question all of life so many times again and

again. You're my man, my creature to love, and I don't care about
a goddamn other thing—

And I make her happy in the way that the sungod would make
a peasant girl happy, descended to earth to do his ritualistic sun
dance and his ray of phallic energy fertilizing and the energy
streaming into the artery of joyous passion and the cries of freed
energy—and it is wonderful, you're right baby, you're absolutely
right, my god, I mean what a fool I've been, and we have a happy
life, and we make love like planets swirling on their axes, and we
thunder and blister and weep with happiness on each other in the
act of love—this is the important thing, not those bitter thoughts
about purpose or the meaning of it all, or why I am here—and so
lucky to have you——but is this right, is it baby, am I right about
all of this strange stuff, this jagged and abstruse theory——

Come here, baby, you just tell Marie why you're upset and tell
me where it hurts, and I'll heal your profound wounds with this
languorous thing called the kiss, and then we'll see how much
your confounded mind has to say about other things—ha, come
here baby, let me show you.

The music of life strums a rich magnificent chord and that's
it, man, the dream lived, and why did I worry . . .

But to see life with new rays—the new light, and the new visions
and portents imparted to me by suprarational things, and again
thinking all over again, thinking about life and why I'm here with
this woman, and what our statuesque beauty when we stand
together naked like models for the great painter, what this is all
about—I can make sense of none of it. Nothing except the lonely
music that produces itself with its own drummer every time I
look a new way—and that ratta tat tat of life's melody and chord
dissonance is the key to another more abstract idea that builds on
itself and builds more—what if I don't understand anything???????

Baby, you frustrate me with all this goddamned worrying—you
get your fun, don't you? why the worrying then? And a low-down

throaty bass hits a funky deep note right then and I'm speechless, can't say a goddamned thing to my woman, who lies there like a coiled sphinx or panther, ready and open and asking and desperate—and I can't answer—and baby I'm so apologetic but I don't think I understand even a goddamned thing about this crazy life or its contingencies, and I want to love you more than anything right now, tonight, but I just don't think I can because I don't really know anything about anything——wife angry wife scorned shoots away and flames rising up and the entire atmosphere charred by a bottomless fury.

I'm sorry baby really.
We won't talk for another couple of days—

Things are really changed, and now I'm saying odd things to my lover like, I dream of touching you, and she smiles sweet smile of sensual attraction and golden fertility grain goodness—we hold each other still, and forget all past disagreements, and all is renewed, and we try to forget what went wrong, where the chasm began. But I sit in the cold empty studio and the loft lofty space and the New York overlooking view, and renew efforts to be productive and not feel guilty that I am sponging off a resplendent lover with money, and we make love and I love the taste of her skin in the mornings—what about painting after all, and am I being babied or what, and what about raging New York down there, and what about sending slides of my work to galleries, or talking to Marie's friend who seems interested in that terrible painting of mine with the red uterus housing the man—what, what? I'm going insane—I try to explain to myself that something's only frustrating me temporarily, one of those evanescent trifles—but something's really eating me alive, and I think I'm hitting that point where I get restless and want to move away and do something, really do something—all of this tragic because Marie—I have to let go of her, or she of me, and the fucking wild frustration of the knotted lump in the throat—I didn't do this, it was my father affecting my neotenic mind when I said I hated you and the dishes weren't done before I washed the floor at the same time that I wanted to make love while you were looking at that brochure and taking off earrings of sexual frustration arising from occasional disinterest in sex because unresolved conflicts with your father and mother who held you in her womb and the ungrateful moving on, leaving me, ahh, how could you guilt-trip me with such mindlessness and the disappointment engendered by your habits, bad idiosyncrasies, and goodbye, don't ever come back I don't love you never did—

W e have been driving for several hours, staring at the white-streaked asphalt stretching before us, which speaks to us in a spiritual way. I'm carrying on a conversation with it. The lovers are behind me, wrapped in a deep tight embrace. They don't say anything but coo and cheep now and again like chicks born in the same egg, and I smile at these moments and look at the highway or road and consider it a friend like any other. There is music in my head, kind soft music—or perhaps it's just their cooing and cheeping. Perhaps I too am in love, though not in the usual sense of the word—love is everywhere for the taking. I just grab it in my hands and yank it towards me. I think we are in

New Mexico somewhere, though I'm not sure. Don't even know what highway or route we're on. I want to talk to the lovers about the highway, their love, the earth and the stones and the motorcycle that passed us not long ago—egoishly, bombastically. That motorcycle too was important, relevant. It was asserting itself angrily, and we took offense at it, and it screamed away happily, having proved itself a part of life. This, I want to say to them, is life in all its fullness. The cowpats rolled and wrinkled up on the fields—the weeds and the gnarled bent pines. Love, earth, the sun faintly coming up to say hello. This is it. A million universes in one—one universe for each part of the greater one. The lovers are their own universe, I am mine, the motorcycle is its own. We are all each other, drifting around each other. Sometimes we collide. The lovers don't really care about a damn thing, and I don't blame them, and they appreciate this. They are fused like snails in the coital act. They are a movie.

In these New Mexican mountains one can't help breathing deeply and letting go of huge chunks of clotted confusion and sadness—that is what I mean by love. Huge bones and teeth of mother earth, bloodstained and dried, red dirt and sandstone and shale and volcanic upthrusting ridges of rugged towering earth-face. Ancient as hell. The air is clean, clean and free. The woods are pungent and nose-itching, and the sun is good and warm on the face and the skin. Never been happier, ever, than this time with the lovers eating potato chips from a 7-Eleven gas station far behind us, necking in the back seat while I drive and lecture on New Mexican eternity and relevance and clouds or earth-teeth jaggedly overshadowing me. What is greatest, if this is great, is knowing how much of life I am swallowing right now, right now now, eating the moment frantically and hungrily—aware through the whole thing how good it is. I'm never forgetting it.

The car putters. We are getting filthy—haven't bathed in a while. Stop every fifteen minutes to unrinate or just stretch our legs. We argue pettily over the climate, or something equally ridiculous. We need somewhere to go. The road becomes insistently maddening once you've been on it for too long. You are driving and getting nowhere except to the next endless stretch of road, and then more road, and the potato chips are sinking in your belly, and the sun is making you sweat—

I know where we can go. My uncle owns a ranch not far from here, and we can go there and rest and stay for a while. Ricardo lives near Dixon past more gigantic ridges of granite or limestone or whatever stones these are.

We stop by a stream just to cool our feet in the water, and the lovers begin kissing again, so I leave them to do their thing, and they don't come back to the car for another half hour. . . . The sun is a blowing ball of embershine that's thrusting through my eyes and mouth, a crushing spiritlove

The water trickling through their armpits downstream
as they kiss
brown leaves rotting in their hair—warm straining wind

I eat potato chips and write down some notes and thoughts in one of the notebooks in the trunk. I love this work. It is palpable spirit stuff inscribed, kept safe. Never lose it. I lived in San Antonio, Texas for a while and used to sit in the parks looking at noonday-playing children and tourists passing in and out, birds, the political activists demonstrating, and I was part of everything, the all-embracing watcher—this is poetry or watching, continuous living, the unexplainable life.

Now we come to the ranch and watch pleasantly-stinking cows sullenly walking and backwards-glancing at us. The fence is hard striated wood, warped and soulful. Out here on the fertilized earth, sinews or ropes of the soul are stretched and momen-

112

tarily pulled out, cords of knotted tension—abruptly, the cows and their shit cut them, so I am let go and I am heavy with fecund earth power.

Ricardo is here, and he seems not at all surprised, rather just interested, so we talk and he touches his hat and moves it around. Sweaty snakes of hair drip under the brim. His eyes are kind and laughing when they look into mine. My mama, he says, misses me, so I ought to get in touch with her. I know, I say. Ricardo is the most unworried soul I know. He is a chunk of old earth and stone singing so slowly as to go unheard except by those who notice his wrinkled smile of brown leather or his boots kicking in the shit of his land, something more precious than gold. Tío, I missed you—*¿que dices, que ha pasado?*/what do you say, what's been happening? He laughs and doesn't say anything. Everything is fine.

The lovers awkwardly drag themselves onto the land of the ranch, ashamed and sheepish and clutching each other. S'okay you idiots, it's only the land and the ranch and cows don't blush or get squeamish. Young cretins. The sky is pure blue exploding before the mind—crows are screeching in its enormity.

Looking with widened eyes at everything lying around me, the land, the blood and life flowing through it—all of my brothers grew up here and all of them have left parts of themselves deeply thrust in the ground. I too have left part of me here, a dark cowpat of anger and bloodrage and soul, the product of all my years and meditations and heartwrenchings. I want to shovel into the earth, digging up the body of my buried heart, just to hold it in my hands and watch the trickling of my own life fluid. But nothing like that can happen. There is no sure way to reconcile yourself with the earth. It simply comes—this reconciliation simply comes of its own will, in its own time. I watch the sun and the mountains and inhale the rich smell of the ranch, laugh with Ricardo, joke about the shy lovers.

The house is compact and warm and yellow. The walls are not straight—they come up irregularly, meeting in obtuse or acute angles at the corners of the rooms. The sofa and the chairs and the table—sinewy rude shapes squatting like animals. There is nothing polished here, but the house is proud. My body sighs. The lovers immediately sit down on the couch and cuddle each other. Piedad, Ricardo's wife, shuffles into the kitchen, warm and dark—she asks me everything and I answer, barely able to keep from laughing with joy. We eat and my head spins . . . happy . . .

When we leave, it is dark and our headlights cut sharply into the shadows. The rock rises sheerly on all sides—we are pushing through the hollow petrified heart of the earth-being. The lovers don't understand or care much about what I'm saying. The girl is beautiful—she looks into the rear view mirror, brushing her thick black hair. Her eyes are gems of light, her eyebrows feathery ridges. The boy chuckles and touches her waist. I force them to talk now—about anything, just to keep our universes in balance. They are drinking warm stale soda and looking out the windows at dry fields and far-off lights of another city. The boy recounts a ghost story—his lover cracks a joke right in the middle of it and we erupt in laughter. His story is ruined. The night is gorgeous. We drive because we long to reach into ourselves and touch our spirits—we want the pounding heart substance of dreams and spirit visions.

After driving for many hours—days really—the difficulty is in grounding, in finding one's roots again and holding onto them. We are driving through the darkness and riding deep churning horses of spirit, clinging to their manes and hollering out for more, deeply drinking the starry night liquor and tasting our blood essence—we have found branching roots, roots stirring powerfully, and we clutch them like triumphant warriors, swing-ing on them. The wood warped by wind and sun—the wood of being, the striae brown and black, the rotten and lovely pith of our brains and our spines and viscera—this too we howl at—this lunacy of self-discovery is what we need and seek—and with each new discovery we run on, hooved and horse-maned, screaming in moonlight and weed-roots, tearing up fresh steaming earth, burrowing down to the heart or the cervix of *madre tierra,* blindly, painfully—until we somehow burst and dreamlike collapse, sleeping on the shoulder of the road in the car, the smell of our unwashed bodies strong——

We pore over *Flesh of the Gods,* searching through blossoming grassy fields for the herbs and seeds of godheaven, avid, intrepid. We want to see and know and never have to stop. The love and sweat of the times cannot be washed off our skins, our pure skins. We burst at the eyes in pinpointed sunflowers of grassy glory—we watch each other like immaculate voyeurs through the translucent space of sky—we conceive the yearning of a worldwide bodytouch together—the vagina of the earth, the penis of turquoise dripping sky—the lubricious jittering of minute life spasms, the lung inhalation of gasping sun breath, the flow of earth onto hands and skin so that temperature is released—motion of tissue, or organ, the brain active and the eyes penetrating—to reach upwards and clasp something greater than self or unself, the utmost realization of internal and eternal peace everlasting to all things, unified with eyes of a million stars or sparks, the love spring and effusion of seeds—the lapsing of sea over our heads and the diatoms that brush, and the flowers that caress, the terrible depth-surging crash into heads until understood, almost overcome—rasping horizontal streak of light. We have seen, we have understood. Quiet. Quiet breathing and fluttery eyelashes. Cheeks. A mole on the back. The flesh. Bellies and lips and inner thighs—I watch them and then sleep.

We have need of more. I read to them of my notebooks—philosophical reveries and dark brain waves recorded with words. Psychotropic flowers pressed between pages of soul writing and pages documenting physical experiences with evidence—like smudges of red earth, locks of hair, twigs from trees, dried tears leaving warped indentations on the paper. The girl puts menstrual blood on one page, the boy semen on another. Writing ferociously about everything at the same time, like a capturing of pregnant butterflies in rapt hunger. The chameleon again—color melting and its eye rolling as skin loosens on the body, until it is entirely loose and free floating around the body, so the body floats in the distended skin like an embryo, and the dark eyes can be seen shifting through the veiny amber sac. Fluid or red energy. Lizard watch. Ochre configurations peering from the inside of rocks to the dry chartreuse dust. The crack of stone in drips of eternal growth. Caves. Eyes. Monstrous vision. The alien beauty of undoing self, unraveling patterns—the physiognomy of porous swollen sensitivity. Can touch. The strumming of light-haired arm, as with a guitar, and the fire song.

Hostilities dissolved. Love paramount——

We loved—kissed
The going of visibility
   sunlight

"So, Flaco, we goin' for a ride or are we?" Lobo is a brother of mine, in a way. He drinks too much and he doesn't have a grip on anything. Now he wants to go for a ride, and I'm such a lonely person that I jump in his old Chevy and holler as it revs and shakes and finally screams off onto the road.

"So, like, why the hesitation, man? Gimme those cigarettes over there, willya?"

I don't say anything. He is a burly chunk of a person. He calls me Flaco because it makes sense to him. I'm thin. And Lobo is life. His gut is enormous. He drinks everything in huge gulps and belches it back out. He clutches his friends in fiendish bear hugs and tries to kill his enemies. Music is his life.

"You remember that chick Rachel? Man, she wus a bad scene. Nearly got killed 'cause a her. Turns out she's gotta boyfriend, and he killed some guy just for lookin' at her."

"Damn."

"Hell yeah 'damn!' I got my ass the hell outta there. California's lookin' pretty good this time a year. Whattya say, hombre?"

"I don't know. I got things on my mind."

"Well start talkin', amigo. We only got all night."

The world is melting and unreal outside, and I'm riding with Lobo right through it, as I've done for years. This is the life. The light is glaring and sharp in front of our eyes. I am a single atom—Lobo and I are a single atom barreling through the void.

The Chevy is neon now, and Lobo doesn't know what's going on. He doesn't see the lights and the emptiness, the gigantic voyage we're making. I ride with my oblivious brother, holding onto his soul, moored to his gut and his strength, his volcanic laugh.

I say, "I fell in love with this girl. It was drippy and sad and all. We weren't even together that long."

"Man, don't even start with me on that. Love ain't nothin' but a pain in the ass. I told you from day one, don't ever get bruised up by some chick who don't look twice at you before you're in bed. Shit. I had enough a that."

"So you've been in love before?"

"Goddamn, brother. Don't you ever listen to me? I wus in love with *Sherry,* long time ago. Damn, she was the most beautiful thing ever walked. Wrote a song for her . . ."

Rev, room, vroom goes the Chevy. The night and the street-lamps hiss and dance. The people outside switch and swing their bodies.

"So then what happened?"

"Damn girl fell in love with some Elvis impersonator or sum shit. I tried ta kick his ass. Huh. Dumbass started ta sing 'Love Me Tender' when I threw a punch. Huh."

I laugh uproariously. Lobo just sits there, a grim block of humanity. He grumbles and tries not to laugh, though inside he knows how funny it all is.

I say, "My girl gave me up for some fag poet."

"I thought you wus a fag poet."

"Well, I am but I try not to show it so you won't get scared."

We throw our heads back and laugh. Lobo forgives me silently, though he fears the *anima,* or femininity in himself or any other man, or anything not at once mighty and macho. For years I have sat in his truck and laughed with him, and wondered at the antithesis of our personalities, and the balance they create in our friendship. If I am a fag and he is a bear, then we laugh at it and go on.

"So uh, whattid ya do?"

"I just told her how much it hurt me, and she didn't care."

Lobo squirms. "Yeah well, if you ever wanna see that dude get roughed up, jus' tell me, man. I'll do a number on him . . ."

Life is a Chevy and the music of its coughing exhaust pipe and our talk.

"So, uh, like what the hell man? Where ya been, Flaco. Chickening out on me?"

"No. Just busy, that's all. I have to focus, you know?"

"Focus?! Shut up with that, man. All I know's music, women and good times. You gots to live and shit for a change, man.

Focus . . . who told you you had ta do that?" We are rolling up a hill, ascending to the top. I am wondering inside whether Lobo will ever realize that I cling to him for protection, that he is my shield. I sit next to him and watch the world, safe. His machismo, for that reason, is not oppressive to me, but a boon, because I hide beneath it and find the opportunity to smile.

From the top of the hill we overlook the entire city, reeling and shimmering like a carpet of broken glass. I spin inside the truck.

"Man, ain't this just it?"

"Yeah, it is, Lobo."

"Man, I brought Sherry up here long time ago. We were in love and everything. Man, I's the happiest guy then. . . . She wus all excited and shit. She really dug me. I's like, 'Baby, you're my sunshine,' and she started laughin,' real happy."

"You really loved her."

"Fuck yeah I did." There follows a long silence, and then he cries a bit, shuddering in big trembling sweeps. His sobs come softly at first, then he bursts out pitifully. Crying, too, for his mother and father—I know this. In a while he will talk about seeing his father strapped to a hospital bed with tubes up his dick and his nostrils, being injected with morphine, dying of cancer. He loved his mother far more than any Sherry, and worships her endlessly, not realizing it. He didn't love Sherry, but the bit of love and kindness she gave him that, for an instant, filled the gap of his mother's missing love.

"I ever show you this?" He produces a small watercolor painting from the glove compartment. It is the portrait of an imaginary woman that he calls Molly.

"Yeah, sure did."

"That's right, you're the guy that always thought this wus real art and shit. Nobody else digs it 'cept you." Molly has lavender hair and black eyes. Her beauty is strange, grim, almost macabre. Mother with curlicues of sperm-like bodies swimming around her sky of hair. She is real to me—that is why I love this painting.

119

"So what you been up to?"

"I think. I think about everything, Lobo."

"Yeah, you and thinking. You jus' worry too goddamn much, man. Shit. That time we wus at that party and you wus stoned and spaced out. You start sayin' all this crazy beat shit and words and go off your rocker, and then you go up to some chick and touch her face and call her goddess and her man nearly knocks the hell outta you. Lucky I wus here ta explain these things, otherwise you'da been history. You just think too much, man. I says to the guy, I says, 'My pal here, he just took some funny tea, he's gone with the wind, you dig?' Man, you are so lucky . . ."

The wind sings. The starshine. Lucid. I love Lobo more than he could know. He has saved me. Has dragged me up from blind black sleep into light and slapped my face and ordered me to *live*.

"Man, 'member that time we wus playin' at this bar, and we wus doin' a slow blues and shit, and when we's finished, we went for a drink—we come back over and the new band's gettin' ready ta play. So we sit back and wait. Then you get up'n say, 'Fuck, that dude's playin' my guitar!' 'You sure?' I ask. 'Yeah, that's *my* guitar,' so we go up there right in the middle a their set 'n innerupt 'em and shit, and we're fightin' over the goddamn guitar, and I'm ready ta off this punk and shit, and then I ask you again— 'cause I ain't so sure—'Is this really your guitar?'—and you look real close and get this funny scared look on your face, and I know, I just know it ain't your goddamn guitar, and real quick I put you behind an' say, 'Like, our fault, man. Real sorry . . .' Man, they woulda smashed you like a bug if I hadn'ta been there. You are so lucky . . ."

He starts up the engine again, and it revs and screeches and down we go, plummeting from the top of the hill over the edge, to the bottom. We both holler as we rush down, reaching our arms out the window, trying to grab the world.

And Lobo says to me, as we're driving down South Broadway, "How about a little rhythm, just like in them good old days?" He is wearing sunglasses, and his hair is long, uncombed, unruly. Music madman devil, son of redsun glories and hot throatsongs, he wants to go get the old equipment and go to an old place where we used to jam, return there and see what kind of scene we can stir up. So we go to his house and load up amps and mikes, his sax, a bass. "I know a drummer we can use tonight," he says. So we screech across town to find this drummer—and he's not there. So we roll back across town and go to our jamming site and hope to find one. Me and Lobo walk in and look around and swing as we walk, and he goes up through the musty smoke-filled place, right up to Hank, and says, "Hey, old cat—lookin' good there—whattya have to say?"

Hank says, "Hey man, where you been? Long time, long time haven't seen ya. So you wanna play again? Got that old fire?"

"Amen, brother. 'Member this old friend a mine?—he's here with me, wants to play."

I don't know how we find a drummer, but we do. We load up the equipment on the small space, stage at the front. And the people are just sitting and staring, remote.

Bass bass bass low thump twang, I start up slow and cool, thumping the bass and the low slow drone—drummer, thin black cat sitting slouched, starts in with quick raps on the snare, hits the high hat. The beat is rap tatta thrump—my bass budoomps and boomps—I'm holding it to me like a woman—Lobo blows faint starting notes squeaking through his dusty silver instrument, peeps falteringly—comes close, bends his body up—upwards reaching and stretching (and this is how he plays, like sucking on the nipple of cosmic rhythmic tit drooping from the sky) and the hollow flooding notes that cry from his bent beautiful sax shiny cold smooth—from inner crying center the bleeping rage of a drunk lovesick musician—*I need ya baby, I wanta be saved, I wantya to hold me and the love, pouring, soul saved—bleep, blu blu breee*—the minute rolling squeals of bursting notes, the honk and doleful bleating and the sad wrinkling of his eyes into tortured motherless criminal's eyes, holding onto that sax body bent upwards, clinging, sweaty arms—

Wild jagged thrum dum budump, lonesome spinning vrrrt blip blaplooooooong howl.

We go on giving our life up in the sweaty devotional music, immortal soul baby   immortal soul

The drummer slams and cracks his skins like a sacrificial cat drawing out claws, his heart thumping up every second, the pitter of subtle beats and the boom of drop beats. Music, music— cleaned and released into night.

Later on we are in a diner, exhausted. Lobo smokes. The light shines on his face, ghostly. Lobo asks me to start a band with him. "We'll go on the road, man. We'll do it." I say nothing. I watch the trembling of his cheeks as he sucks on the cigarette. His eyes are depthless brown—his arms are huge, tattooed. "Whattya say, amigo?" He tells me I'm the only other one who's got what's needed. "Me and you," he says—"we'll go here and there and do chicks and gigs and make soul music. . . ."

We eat a little. We sit and stare. Lobo discusses life in his foul visceral way. Love and night. We remember old loves, and we look at the night. There is nothing else.

The first thing you knew about him was that he was bleeding in sync with the times, the generation, and his every word and breath was the essence of all young expectant waiting watchers like you. And he could saunter over to you while you sat and know what you thought and with a strange magic twitter of the eyes tell you everything you needed to hear. And his hypnosis was spiritual and like a winding turning staircase that brought you down to dark rooms of that part of yourself that you ordinarily would have avoided. He was a walker and a talker—he looked like a foreign unshaven poet and all of those necessary things— yes, he was it. He was the core of the serpent god or the truth god or the wisdom king, to whisper in your ear, to make you reel and think again, *Who is this person.* But you knew who he was. It was him.

He was wearing a dirty tie-dyed shirt the first time you saw him, under a tweed coat, and his jeans were ragged and thread-bare. He smelled of the road life, grasses and cigarettes and things that you vaguely smell when you leave for the first time the threshold of your parents' house. This one had seen it from the old times to the new times, and he had exchanged words with the greats and the nobodies, he knew what the precise value of words was. He could tell you everything from the first chapter of life to the grand finale, all with the greatest coolness and unblinking passion. And then he would squint and light up and thoughtfully caress the smoke, and you knew what masterful hands those were that he had, soft and unique, careful not to press too much or hold back in any way. He would sit back and watch, diving through time, and after a long silence he would jerk back with some shocking prize that struck your deepest nerve—you had *known* this person was there, you had known that he was *somewhere,* only you couldn't talk about him the way you could anything else, and you were afraid to bring him up. He was sacred and dangerous and beautiful. Your parents would never understand him, and the professors were nothing next to him, and flowers were just waiting to reach over and become enmeshed in his coat.

And you wanted to suck his lips, hear him speak because that was all that mattered. You waited for the reaching of his hands over to your shoulders, the stare of his eyes, his rippling wind of words. He could rhapsodize about you and love and truth or untruth and the seeds of thought or time, and this made you itch and hum. Quickly you were following his every squeaky step with worn tennis shoes—quickly you were stumbling after because you wanted more, more, and could never stop wanting—that was what distinguished him from any other laughing devil lover that you'd known or had. You couldn't turn around in the middle and laugh. He was rough and sensitive and he was the wind and the sea—he could uproot trees of pain and he could set free storms of glory all in a second with a glittering flash of handsome teeth behind reddish smiling lips with brown hairs growing above them. He could extend hands to you and the world and talk about what lay out there, knowing exactly what he was talking about—he just threw out his palms and talked about Texas or Ohio or rivers or mountains—the trees and their creatures. Or he could say with utter certainty that today you were a romantic or a sorrowful waif—every time he was right, every time he had crawled inside of your body and looked closely at your patterns or hieroglyphs, and read them back to you. You loved him. You would have died for him, simply because he was salvation, a saint, holy where others were crude, certain where others weren't. He didn't have ideas, he wasn't out to understand any more. He knew and he loved, and he had faint trails of hair running down his cheeks, burning lengths of sideburn, and his brief touch on your arm was a flame of hell called up to make you rush infinitely.

"But why," you would ask, "but why me, and why these kisses and touches and words . . . do you love me?" And he was Pan himself laughing with you or at you, and who could say which? But then he was springing up and dragging you away to feasts of wine and truth, and he brought you books and images like they had been yours all along, and he clutched everything without fear—the man playing a harmonica, the Marxist haranguing for dear life, the cars flashing by angrily—these were all real spirits that he could embrace and put into understandable light. And he sang low lovely hymns for you out of nowhere, and you cried for mercy because it was so huge and unbearably good. When could it stop? He met your foolish English professors on their own terms, defeated them with their own words, wrote books of frantic nonsense that reorganized and unhinged entire societies—he stormed here and there and sweatily jumped into conversations, snapping at people, shutting them up so well, truthfully, a man of song and truth, with the roar of the sea behind him and all those things you had sat up late at night dreaming of. There was a sweet satyr-like virility in him, there was such assertive beauty— perhaps you loved him because you wanted that in yourself, or you saw your own reflection. But he made these things petty with crashes and booms of sea and understanding, or the hair that brushed you when he kissed your face.

He could stand there next to you while you waited for the bus, and coax you out of bitter anger because you had seen him with a girl—and he was so delicious it made you forget. Because he was showing you new things, and you were young, and he showed this to you patiently, and you loved your own good beauty, and you stayed, aware of the fact. And you noticed he was buying you trinkets to hang from an earlobe, spices to spread over your skin. He showed you a flower radiating within and then quietly watched as you looked and saw the way it was.

But only a long time later would you see him stumble back over the raw hills of his life into that sorry patch where he was born, stumbling back over ages and myths and all of his lovers into the hen's nest of home. And when this happened, you knew he was a boy who was rough and cold and like sea stones in their insentience—a boy who loved his grotesque mother and slept in a shabby room with chickens and lizards, who read too much and tremendously, and from early age had sensed his distance from life, and so decided he was going to master it. And he did. And he became everything that you had needed him to be and that all the sunken souls had needed him to be, but inside he didn't care, and was faun-like laughing at you and his tricks. You loved him and his dizzying words, but they were nothing. Nothing at all.

There was one blue room with expanding cubes of light on the walls above rough dried canvases and the red crooked assemblages on the floor. "It could be a gallery," I said.

"It's not. It's a studio." This he said with a laugh, explaining himself to a boy, to me. I felt young and ignorant next to him. "But I'll tell you," he said, "there aren't too many spaces left around here for everyone. People need places to go, places to unite, if you know what I mean."

"Yes," I said, though I meant no. The room was cold and frightening. We waited for cold grey moments there, shifting onto different feet, looking at his works. I wanted to leave, chewing my nails. It was not a place to be with clear sensitive eyes. One needed to come in here having seen enough, been shocked enough. He was short and hunched and obdurate next to me. He had been working in here for a long time, in the cold, hammering together browning photographs and tacking together pieces of life. He had run in here and closed the garage door on the sunlight and begun smearing cold ugly thoughts in what he called art. It was his need. I couldn't understand a person of his nature—I wanted to ask how he could do it, just sit here and do it, but he looked at me without anything in his eyes that suggested he wanted to hear my question. "What now?" I asked.

He laughed again. "Let's go outside," he said.

It was an ugly square of cement and wooden fence outside. There were spiny plants with purple flowers at the fringes. How could he live here? There was nothing, no one, no life. I think he somehow created his own. I wanted to be direct now, and ask what I wanted. "Do you get lonely out here?"

"Out here? . . . What does that mean?" Now he was shifting from one foot onto the other, without socks.

"I mean, out here away from many people."

His laughter at my question was raucous. "There're neighbors," he said. Then: "I don't know what you mean by lonely. I got work, I got space. That's all I need. People come at night."

"Really?"

"All the time. This isn't just my pad. When people come at night, things happen, you know?" He was smiling, and I knew then that he *was* lonely, regardless of nighttime visitors.

I asked, "People like who?"

"You've got lots of questions. You don't really understand this scene, do you?"

I shook my head. The draft whisked sidewalk dirt.

"Well, I'll try to explain it to you. To explain this, I've got to say that nothing before the fifties was important, except a few people. I didn't know this at first, of course. When I was about your age, I guess, in art school, I didn't know how much shit they were feeding me with their classicism. It's about expression, nothing else. Don't let anyone tell you different, man. But anyway, I didn't know anything about anything, at first. I started out being just a dumb kid. I didn't want to be an artist. I don't think I wanted anything."

"What did you do?"

"What did I do? It was real easy going at first, your run-of-the-mill art school deal, but then I met them."

"Them?"

"Yeah, them. I can't explain it any other way. They were there, man. People, people who wanted to live and get drunk on it all. They weren't out to theorize or explain it, the way I'm doing now. They *lived.* You dig jazz?"

"Yeah."

"Well, then you know what I mean. Once I saw what was real, I couldn't stand art school. So I left, you know? Just left and went with 'em. But it didn't just happen like that . . . well, I guess it did. It was just *Bam*, and then I was gone."

"Where did you go?"

"Where? Everywhere. Think about your wildest dreams—the really wild ones—and then imagine that one day you were so excited you started living them. I mean, it was unbelievable, but you knew it was happening, and so you believed it, man, did you *believe* it." He paused and shuffled his cold feet. "But that was only the beginning, man, it got weirder and crazier and fuller. Imagine everyone you know or consider important involved in life with their entire gut behind it. Imagine them doing their damndest to grab life in their hands and arrest it and put it down somewhere. People live this way. Excited isn't a decent word for it. It's an amazing burst of your secret ideas—if you can imagine art going on for centuries and eons without getting anywhere, and then bursting, just bursting out of the sky into everyone's lap and waking them up—then you understand this."

He was like a monk. We returned to his studio after a short time. He sat down and took blankets around his own shoulders, his hair looking like a mass of broken feathers.

"So what do you think?" he asked.

128

"About what?"

"I don't know, life, art, things in general."

I wanted to say something important, as grand and true as his jazz oration, but he sat and looked like a crow, and I could say nothing. "Well?" he said.

"I can't think of anything to say."

"Don't think about it! Just say it. Blurt it out. You'll see, once you say it, you'll find out what's true and what's not."

For a while I was angry, brooding while I sat.

"Look," I finally said. "You don't need to treat me like some conservative foreigner who ain't hip to your artistic truth. I'm scared, okay? I'm not dumb, I'm scared. What am I doing here anyway? Half the bullshit you've been talking about I already knew. I didn't wake up yesterday. I'm hungry, I want to know, I want to be alive, like you were saying."

He laughed. "That was pretty good there, kid. I'm jealous. I didn't care about any of this until a few years ago. I applaud you!" He clapped maniacally, and I couldn't help laughing. He was, after all, a lonely strange man. I liked him after a while. "Want some soup?" he asked.

We went into the dingy kitchen where he began heating up a can of soup. There were ants on the table. Something about his place was still frightening; somehow it was too potent in its stillness, too aggressive even in its silence.

"Life is crazy," he said. "Beautiful, too. . . . You're lucky you came to California and not, say, New York. People here commune with each other—there it's cold. But the greatest thing is the people here have all decided they're going to live. Even death is a part of life—so they don't let that stop them. Do you know what that means? Art has never meant so much . . ."

The soup was runny. I watched him eat peripherally. He sucked down the soup as if it were marrow. Afterwards he shuddered and sighed.

"Yes, when I was your age, I guess, I was learning things that couldn't be explained—the things that you're learning. The *experience,* the *experience*—that's the most important thing! That's what they can't teach you in any goddamned art institute. Everywhere I looked, every side of the world, there was art and genius and it was manifesting itself like you wouldn't believe. I mean, you had only to walk out into the street and you were fertilized—your head spun and your germinal spirit woke up and exploded and grew shoots that sprang out. No one stood and commented on it. . . . Man, it *happened.* People didn't scribble poetry, or make drawings—they turned them out like devils and cried and watched their most gigantic nightmares crawl out of them—they were engines of life grinding away in madness, and that's how those people learned to live after so long a time of not living. Do you know what this means?"

And his eyes gleamed and his hands were clenched with sincere fervor. "It means everything!"

He slouched back and crossed his arms. Slowly he uncrossed them and spoke. "I used to know how to gamble, if you can believe that. I was just a kid, and I thought I knew what I was doing. I used to behave like a man and carry myself like a man, but I was just a kid—I mean a real kid, like fourteen. That was how old I was when I had my first sexual experience. It was with this girl Susanna. I didn't know what I was doing, but I went up to her and said, 'I'm going to be perfectly honest, because life is too short not to be. I need you. I need you.' It sounded good to my ears, and it must have sounded good to hers, too, because we

130

made love. But what I had said—it was true. It had been absolutely true. Then I forgot all about this, only thinking that I had been doing what a man does or maybe this experience was what made me a man. But then a long time later I remembered it—my absolute honesty with this girl, and what came of it. That's what it's all about. You live from your gut—you live from your heart. That's why I came here. That's why I paint. People stop doing this—being honest, being true to their innermost needs and drives—and they dry up and blow away. If you haven't got passion, you haven't got art or life."

Abruptly he scuffled out into the adjoining room, where there were paintings and assemblages. He motioned for me to follow. He stood in front of one piece that was constructed like an altar with a primitive wooden goddess icon at its top. He stood there, shivering and mad, awake, alive.

There was one board at the top of your house, on the roof, that creaked and creaked as if there were someone upstairs in the attic rummaging around through old chests of clothes— this was your fear, your assumption, which you clearly stated through a fit of laughs. You talked about old grandfather and his clothes upstairs and what importance those old things had. And his hands, you said, had been like chapped paintings of green and blue dried oils. And his eyes, you said, had been like muddied and leafy puddles—just like those outside, waiting to freeze over right now. And we talked and talked over warm cups of things which we drank, and you sat with legs folded under you and looked outside through the window, and seemed hollow and full at the same time, full of immense feeling that couldn't be verbalized. Talked and talked. I loved the walls and the ceiling and the creaking, the worn rug, the storm forming outside. When it snows, you said, I'll bring the children in. The children were outside kicking up cold leaves and sticks, waving their arms and searching and foraging. The snow was trying to come in, come down. We talked, then, about your crummy apartment, not yours any more, situated in the most desolate half of town, and who must be in it now. This house was much better, you said. You moved quickly up and talked on the phone and were gone for a while. There was one bed against which I leaned and on which one of your children slept every night—we were sitting in the living room and since there were only two bedrooms, one bed had to be in there instead of out in the snow or up in the attic, creaking like some grandfatherly stranger hungry for old relics.

You returned. The snow isn't coming yet, you said. You looked wistfully out the window again, and began the talk, the talk of life. The colors again. It was either green or orange, you said. And everything could be either green or orange, in fact, everything was. I was bluish orange, you said, full and looking as though the paint had been applied with great squeezes of the tubes and then spread around with some kind of flat tool. A spade.

Your garden. There was frozen corn, and brilliant vegetables with hanging skins and brown leaves like limbs. The scarecrow was a family member sitting on a stump next to kind tomatoes. Your children laughed outside. Your voice was dim.

There were books. Finnish poetry and histories of Slavic migrations. Haiku. Many histories. You were history and there was

132

oldness in our motions and every time you spoke you recalled some guiding river or patch of mud that our grandfather had brushed off his shoe. Grandfather was history, and he had a hoe or a treasured garden implement. We were in another room now. I could still remember the other one. I could feel my back against the bed in there, and I could smell the rug. A gift from the former resident, who was your friend. Fairly good friends. You often talked and she loved your children, but then moved to Denver. There is the cold, you said, and remembered the storm, and thought of bringing in the children. But by then they were stroking the scarecrow's hoary beard of wood, and the gloves on his hands, blue, and his orange painted boots. Enamored of the dead corn. There were more things. Divorce, which you talked about calmly, speaking like a magazine article, having learned what divorce meant from magazines. The house inside was warm and the beds waited for bodies and we sat on the rug in the other room, meditatively.

The first child opened the door and icily walked in. Sang a mumbling song about the couple in the restaurant, and walked into the kitchen to drink water, walked around in tapping boots and winter coat. The feeling was the same. What we understood was the motion of mouths, though not the things they spoke. The hard silence between sentences. The hands brushing jackets or sweaters and curling around cups. You waited for grandfather, though the creaking had stopped and was a dripping now, of melting ice. Perhaps there is no storm, I said. No, I read it somewhere, I just know. I watched.

Your child had got penicillin last year for strep throat, which was sore and red, and there were other things to be remembered. The measles. My father, I said, carried me into the bed when I had chicken pox and safely guarded my weakness. He read to me the Anasazi history, which calmed the ruddy itching. It was safe then. And when my penis itched he told me stop scratching it. Since then nothing has really changed, has it, I said, the illnesses are the same and the silence and the calm the same. We are still full. There was the heath outside and the storm coming foggily. We spoke about the lisp of sea and the froth that bathed the rocks. There was a house on the coast just sitting there, waiting to be bought, you said, and I would have, if I'd had the money. The sea was cold and you couldn't see anything except gray out there and I would have given up so much just to live near it. There was once, I said, a time when I collected crab skeletons and fish remnants just to proudly show them to people, what I had collected, the fins and the smelly spines. Things from the sea. I meant to write a book about it and explain to people about carcasses and where they might have been. Then the sand got washed over and I was more interested by the smoothness. Yes you said. A dance, really, I said, if you consider it that. We drank.

I was unhappy in that other place, you said. I had grown up near it and there was nothing for me except the wearing of clothes or the new earrings borrowed from friends, and I couldn't stand it, not another minute of it. I watched cars to see where they went and the new places were real to me, so alive. I moved when I could, fast. There is nothing more for me there. We looked at the window, then out it, and knew what it was to move on, to grasp a new rug or rocking chair or creaking attic and call it new, or mine or yours. So it's better now, I asked. Jesus, you said, and smiled. Can't you tell? What about your old friends, I asked, what about them? What do you say to them? And you said nothing, and that meant you didn't say anything to them. It was getting cold. There was food stored downstairs, water flowing in the pipes. The warmth was needed, or else the damp cold would touch us.

A year before now I was living in a place like this, I said, and the chairs were the best because I had painted them all myself and it was simple but nice. I don't mean what you think I mean, because I was impoverished, and there was no way I was going to do something outstanding. We could go out into the garden, you said. Cold weather, even in bundled jackets. The children were shouldering and jouncing with sounds of joy. Are you waiting for something, I asked. You said no, just breathing, or taking it all in. Garden patches under the feet. There was a frozen something bleeding in the ice. I think the storm is coming, you said.

Your joy, I said, is the most wonderful thing, because it touches what is not ordinarily touched. And the leaves and branches are the kindest in this place. We went inside. Warmth in great gusts. We were flushed, the children gasped and threw boots and muddy galoshes.

This time we sat down with some firmness and seemed determined to talk about unknown things, as if before it had been too silent. I was trying so hard, I said, to be something I clearly wasn't. Machine or automaton. There was never any room for expansion of ideas. It was hard, you said. We talked about the past like past lives. Gone things. There is no correctness, you said, in what is natural, and what seems to have happened is that you corrected what was natural. I released tears. I squinched and squinted, and could not quell this. There is blue on your face, you said.

1993 At home on York Street, San Francisco

I remember when Tiko moved into the apartment below me with his mother—a bright, engaging boy navigating the Mission district with radiance and spirit. And then he became a young man, soaring to heights I would never have expected, inspiring us all. I miss him and his hopeful message.

—John Reamer

1997 Boogaloo's Restaurant, San Francisco

On the day of the memorial service, Itzolin's roommates from Yale (the ones who could make it to San Francisco) sat around my laptop and re-read a bunch of the emails he had sent us over the previous five years. They offered an incredible, hilarious mix of crazy stories (things that could only happen to him), joyous vulgarity, made-up words, pop culture commentary (often with his trademark malapropisms), reminiscences (he was our chronicler at Las Vegas for New Year's 2000), and his own brand of philosophy.

Itzolin was like a brother. He was huge, larger than life, and without a doubt the most brilliant and fascinating person I will ever know.

—Benjamin Carp

Itzolin's Answers to Early-2000s Online Questionnaire:

IF YOU COULD BUILD A HOUSE ANYPLACE, WHERE?
A simple wooden house by the beach. I would paint it turquoise, red and purple. I wish it was the coast of Veracruz, but to be real, somewhere South of the Bay Area where I am not too far away from everyone but the beaches are warm.

FAVORITE ARTICLE OF CLOTHING?
A white t-shirt that has a green frog with red sun rays behind it, it's an image from the Mexican game Loteria. My father painted the shirt by hand and just kept it around, but we always traded clothes, so I ended up with it.

A FAVORITE CHILDHOOD MEMORY?
I was 9 years old, mama was driving me, Cielo and Karina home from school in her VW bug. She had an 8-track stereo and she was playing Bob Marley, Is this Love. We crossed the Rio Grande and it was getting dark, the sun was setting.

WHAT MAKES YOU REALLY ANGRY?
Big people kicking small people when they're down. Vivan los Zapatistas! I'm trying to go to Chiapas this summer, we'll see how it goes.

FAVORITE RESTAURANT OR EATERY?
A taqueria in the Mission that has early 1900s style: wooden posts, clay pots, everything is shadowy. They serve real horchata with whole cinnamon sticks in it. You can order burritos de nopal (the soft part of the cactus). The water is cool and fresh, your heart is filled with mystery, and guitars are singing quietly.

THE ONE PERSON FROM YOUR PAST YOU WISH YOU COULD TALK TO?
I don't think that way. I wish I could have all of my friends and family live in one community in a rural place that is 20 minutes from a major city. Whenever you guys are ready, okay?

138

Thumbs up! Date and photographer unknown

When I think about Itzolin, it's the light he gave off that sticks in my mind. Whether he was sharing something beautiful or making everyone laugh with play fighting or a monologue replete with hilarious facial expressions, he just radiated light. That's what I most remember, and what I most miss.

—Kezia

2000 With sister Oraibi Karina, San Francisco

4/9/01

Itzden,

¿Que tal? I hope you are doing well. You've been in my prayers, as always.

Here's the check for $300.00. Please don't feel bad for accepting it. I'm happy to help you out, carnal.

Call me soon to let me know how everything's going. I tried to call you and Papi on Saturday, but the line was busy every time I called.

I love you so much, baby. May God bless you in abundance.

Tu hermanita que te quiere mucho,

Karina

141

2001 Itzolin's 26th birthday, San Francisco

The first time I met Itzolin was the last time. His smile and warmth from that day have stayed with me ever since. When my choir toured the West Coast I met with my relatives in San Francisco. I will never forget when Tito took out his guitar, played it, and we sang in Mia's kitchen. We also got a big laugh out of it that Tito kept saying, when we got a bit lost driving around, "Just keep going Straight," and we found our way. Just keep following the road, and that's exactly what I'm going to do, just keep going forward, but always remember him. He truly touched my heart. *Hvil i fred Itzolin, jeg vil alltid huske deg og ditt smil, til vi møtes igjen!*

—Mari Dubedåre Ravndal

2001 With sister Shifra

I think about the way he laughed, almost a squeaky breaking of the voice sometimes as if he couldn't help the giggle. He loved to make everyone laugh.

—Shifra Pride Raffel

2002 Turquoise jewelry

Itzolin used to love to see me in a turquoise rebozo I'd drape over myself during my Stanford days. He told me it enveloped me in protection, protección I probably needed on a campus that seldom felt like our home. I can clearly hear him saying, *La turquesa es claridad y harmonia*/Turquoise is clarity and harmony. I still wear turquoise almost daily, and I often think of him and so many things we shared together in the span of our three-year friendship. To this day when I pray or write or dream about him, I reflect on how, like turquoise, Itzolin was powerful, geometric, complicated and infinite. Itzo, movimiento de obsidiana, Obsidian Movement, was one of the first male friends I had who modeled a different type of Chicano masculinity—so vulnerable and open and artistic and sensitive. Because I was used to Chicano men who were machistas and abusive, sometimes his openness scared me. I remember being taken aback when he first emailed me, seeking me out purposefully for a pure, blissful friendship full of mutual love and respect without pretentions or self-interest. Damn, I miss my friend. A renaissance Chicano, Itzolin was an old soul who carried himself as if most of his actions and words were intentional. Because they were. "¡P'urhepecha de color turquesa! ¡Mi amiga Erandi! ¡Que vivas tu!" I can still hear him shout from the entrance of Centro Chicano. He was alive before Xicanx existed, but if he would have understood today's term as genderless, open-hearted and still invoking an old way of thinking, I think it would have fit him well. *I still wear turquoise, Itzo. I wore turquoise to say goodbye to you at your service in San Francisco and also when Cherrie Moraga held a sweat lodge in your honor.* I know his path was full of turquoise and when he looks back towards those he left in this earthly realm, it is the color that continues to reflect his spirit.

—Gabriela Spears-Rico

Itzolin Audiotape Excerpts

Apples and Flamelight

My earliest memory is of a room in a dusty house with wooden boards and a screen door, and my mom was cooking.

I remember us living on Arno Street in Albuquerque. Arno was kind of a bad scene but a nice street, and we lived in an apartment that had two stories. The building was yellowish, and we lived at the top. A lot of cool things happened up there. I remember well that my mom made me troll dolls. This blue one—it had a red mouth—we left somewhere, and they brought it back. My papi showed it to me, and I had my doll back.

And one time we came home and were walking up the stairs, and my dad stopped. It was a dramatic moment. He had his hand in a certain gesture, like *Everybody hold on.* He put this look of *We've got to be quiet listeners now.* And he said, "The house has been broken into"—so we ran up the stairs. It was a big deal, our house had been broken into, and they had taken a bunch of stuff. The funny part is I remember my dad saying they took meat from the freezer.

And then my mom burned some incense, and I remember her telling me that it was going to make everything okay. And I thought that was so beautiful, you know, 'cause I believed her. Believed she had this magic power to make everything okay. So I was very happy about that.

Then I have a memory on Arno Street where my sister and I were sitting outside, and I had a black floppy hat. My mom used to make these really colorful clothes for us. I remember telling Cielo something in a cowboy drawl, like "Hey, sid daowwwnn."

My mom didn't let me watch much TV, and I pretty much agree with her that it was bad to watch regular TV—my friends would turn it on, and I thought "Little House on the Prairie" was the only good program.

There was a Mexican boy downstairs I played with. My Spanish was pretty good, because that's what we spoke, but I could tell they had a more formal way of talking. I felt a little ashamed.

I also have a very early memory that Jim Cody, my father's friend from college, came to visit. I was in his truck. It was raining, and the windshield wipers were making a shape like two turtles. When one of them would go the other way—when the windshield wiper would flick back—it would crush the shell of the turtle. I got a lot of pleasure from seeing the turtle undone and then redone. Remade.

We used to go to protest ceremonies. This was in the days of the Chicano movement, and lots of things were happening back then—it was everybody's day of creativity and solidarity. It was kind of like the turtle, being undone and redone, everybody in a creative flow. We went to a protest about WIPP, the waste isolation power plant. We drove up there with Velia Silva in the back of the truck. It was seriously windy, and we put a blanket on top of us. I remember sleeping. And when we got there, lots of people were doing music and theater, and we camped out in a green tent.

I don't remember this, but apparently I used to go and read at the poetry readings. I would say things about serpents and ad lib. Just go for it. I had absolutely no sense of shyness. Alan Marks told me once that he heard me extemporize. That I kept saying, *"Zorra, zorra."* This word for fox. *"Y la zorra."* I remember the style. I liked the way the adults read, and I would free-flow off of that. . . . *"Y hay una serpiente en la tierra que va por el cielo. Y abre su boca y come el sol."* [And there's a serpent in the earth that goes to the sky. And it opens its mouth and eats the sun.]

We moved to a house on Lovato, a really nice street, and I remember driving back through there and seeing murals that Mike Epiotis did. We lived in this house that had a wall covered with morning glories, something kind of Aztec, to have a wall covered with flowers. I felt lucky, because that house had a very wild back yard. I loved to play games like I was like a hunter or traveler, or some kind of prehistoric human. And my father would join with me. We had our own language, kind of like Nahuatl, one of the pre-Columbian languages. He would point to the sun: "Isch latchh! Isch lactchh kloosh. Isch gatu ging ga." And I would have a spear. We would go running through the trees, and we called it *el monte*. And berries, mulberries—I would go eat them.

I remember a lot about Cielo. It was so much fun back there, you know? Cielo would play with me, and she wandered around with a little dress like a skirt pulled up over her chest, but it would slip down like a skirt. Like little wild kids, we would run around, and I loved the weeds 'cause they were so tall, taller than I was. It was a very enchanted place that I grew up in then. And Cielo was my sister, my fellow adventurer. I loved Cielo so much. She was my closest companion. We didn't really need to speak to each other.

One time I left her near an ant pile, and she got the crap bitten out of her by all these ants. I felt so bad—we had to put her in the sink and put baking soda on her—she had red spots.

I loved my mom. I remember waking up early in the morning, about six, and asking her to make a tortilla. A hot tortilla for me. Or she'd bring me an apple, and I would curl up in bed next to her. My mom was the one that spoke to me in Spanish at home. More than anybody. I remember the dictionary she made for me. She drew pictures, and it had all these words in Spanish.

My parents had taught me a little about Nahuatl or pre-Columbian images, and symbols and glyphs. I knew the spiral was important, and I also knew about my name and the symbol of movement, which was an *ollin*. My mom said that I used the word *ollin* to mean movement. She said I bumped my head once when I was very small, and when she asked me what happened, I said *ollin*.

149

I remember going with my father one day to the river, and we went to look at the crows. When we came back I wrote in a little journal and did drawings. It felt like a novel, so intense. I loved dinosaurs, and I knew all their names. I used to call the tongues *un espiral,* a spiral. I put a little spiral in the mouths of all the dinosaurs.

I think one of the happiest times of my life was when we were living in that house on Lovato. We had a party for Cielo's second birthday, with visiting family and a lot of neighbors. We dug a pit to roast a pig the day before, to make *barbacoa.* Everybody was digging, and my father was going to take a turn. I was very proud of my father. So I put my arms out, and I yelled, *"¡Y ahora viene el hombre mas fuerte de todo!"* You know—"And here comes the strongest man of all." Everybody laughed at me, and I thought, "That's weird. . . . Why? I mean, he *is* the strongest man of all."

This Colombian friend of the family was there, Fernando, who I thought was cool, because he wore a leather ring around his arm that had a tooth or a horn, kind of an obsidian spike. I don't remember seeing the pig go into the pit, but I had a spear, and I was chasing Cielo with it. When Fernando saw me, he took the spear and immediately put it on the ground, put his boot on top of it, and broke the tip off. He said, "That's dangerous." And he said, *"Y tu puedes correr mas recio que Cielo, porque tu tienes las piernas mas largas."* [You can run faster than Cielo, because your legs are longer.] But I was so pissed at him: *"¡Fernando! ¡No!"* Because he broke my spear.

That night I think my tía and tío were there. I danced with some cousins. The pork tasted so good. It was strange meat, so soft and so tender. When you pulled it away from the pig, you could feel all the fibers of the muscle. I just relished it.

Then I remember a visit with my grandparents, my mom's parents. I really liked Bestie because she would pretend that food was an airplane and my mouth was the hangar. "Ooaaahhh," and she would put the food in my mouth. At one point I had to pee, and in the bathroom, she pulled my pants all the way down. I insisted on doing it my own way. I was humiliated, but I loved her.

I hated preschool [Head Start], 'cause I got shy around kids. I remember learning the ABC's, and feeling weird around a bunch of kids I didn't know. But one day riding on the little preschool bus—I think I had a bloody nose—the driver passed a napkin, and everybody did this motion to pass it back—like seeing everybody move in time with each other. A rhythm!

I did have some trouble at school. Once I wanted to play with a toy phone, and this girl told me very sharply that I couldn't. I was like, "Well, that's silly. You're not using it, so . . . I think it's my turn." I took the phone, and she came over, got this insane look on her face, and she pinched my lip. It started bleeding. And I started to cry. Nothing had ever prepared me for that.

It's hard to explain what it was like growing up in New Mexico, because in Albuquerque we had a small community. Everybody knew everybody, and there were lots of people I grew up with. We *did* things together. You spend time with them, then you don't for two years, and then again it's like family. That's how it was with people like Rosina and Lolita. Lolita's at Stanford now. I knew Greg since I was seven. And other kids I went to school with, Chicanos, or I guess they would call themselves Hispanics.

I went to Armijo for a while, the elementary school in our neighborhood. Sometimes my dad would take me to school on his bicycle—he put a special wooden plank on it so I could. We used to ride by the *acequia*—the ditch. Kids would see us—they would run along the fence separating the ditch from the schoolyard, to follow us.

I found it a little hard to fit in at school, because my parents never taught me about roughhousing. I used to read the encyclopedia at night, just chill up in my bed and read. I remember being seriously confused by a lot of other kids' behavior . . . the rituals, the way they would interact. Two guys or girls would square off and mouth off to each other:

"Make a move then."

"I know you are, but what am I?"

"All talk, no action."

But though I wasn't quite in the same world as my neighbors, I did all right. The first theater production I was in was a play called *Sí Hay Posada,* a comforting story about finding lodging and companionship during Christmas. Marcos Martínez was one of the big presences, and Angie Torres. We rehearsed a lot. I was supposed to be a brat in the play, acting up, and an adult actress had to pull my hair to reprimand me. But in one performance, she pulled my hair so hard I actually cried during the play.

Next stage was Longfellow Elementary School, I think third grade. I was happy. I had done theater with Irene Oliver-Lewis, and I think she was the reason I got in. My father wanted me to be a well-rounded person, so he exposed me to writing and drawing and Aztec dance and then theater.

When my father and I would ride on the *acequia,* we used to see this peacock, and my father would call it *el pavo real,* peacock. It would make this certain sound—"Uh-*uhh!* Uh-*uhh.*" My father and I would sing its song together. And I loved that peacock. It was a male, and it was very beautiful. All those colors.

I was part of an Aztec dance troupe, Xinachtli. I used to go with Lauro Silva on trips to Las Cruces, another part of New Mexico, to do dancing. That whole thing was led by Andrés Segura, who was kind of my spiritual instructor—the one who baptized me in the Nahua tradition. Somewhere I have the clay pot that held the paint he painted me with when he baptized me.

There was a young lady, strong and very lively, Chicana, and we went with Lauro all the way to Mexico City together when I was about seven. We were all camped out, because we had been doing Aztec dancing, and it must have been about four in the morning. I had a dream that I was inside of her—my whole body was inside of her . . . but as if her body was empty, and instead of her internal organs, there was just this large space. There was light inside, and I could see her spine illuminated. I felt a tingling sensation over my whole body.

[Singing] Voy en busca de un mariachi a Garibaldi
Por que quiero darle una serenata
A una prieta que con su desden me mata
Y por ella yo me quiero emborrachar

Aunque mi voz no sea lo bastante buena
Quiero que oiga lo que traigo aquí en el pecho
Esta noche me le planto a lo derecho
Aunque no quiera me tiene que escuchar

Ahora, mariachis, toquenle fuerte
Pa' que me abra las puertas del alma
Ahora, mariachis, toquen querido
Pa' que escuchen mi corazoncito
Que está latiendo muy despacito
Que está latiendo muy despacito

I have a lot of memories of Mexico City. We were in the *zócalo* [main square] and it was an Easter thing. I remember throwing eggs filled with confetti . . . everybody was throwing eggs in the streets. I remember buying pottery. We ended up in a little pueblo and stayed there a couple of days. An older girl—fourteen or something—was *so sweet* to me, her arms around me, taking care of me. When we had to depart, she was saying, *"Adios."* And in front of all her friends I said, uh, *"¿Y qué? No me das un beso?"* What about a kiss? And she was embarrassed. But she did. A kiss on the lips. I think I was seven.

I remember doing *danza* in the *zócalo*. We were doing a ceremony and had to stay up for three nights, and of course everybody had to sacrifice. That was the Aztec way. At one point I was like *This is too much for me,* so I passed out in my sleeping bag. Finally I had to come out and do the *danza*.

There were a lot of *capitanes* there, *capitanes de la danza,* the Aztec dance. It was all day. At one point, everybody was getting their chance to lead. And one of the *capitanes* looked at me and said, *"¿Tu quieres dar la danza?" o lo que sea* [Do you want to give the danza? or something like that]. We had rehearsed a lot, and I remember there being this dance of the sun that I really liked.

BUM bum BUMP bum BUMP bum BUMP bum
BUMP bum BUMP bum
Buda buda BUM
BUM bum BUMP bum BUMP bum BUMP bum
BUM bum BUM
Buda buda BOOM
Buda buda BUMP bum
Buda buda BOOMP boom
Buda buda buda buda buda buda buda buda BUM
Buda buda BUMP bum
Buda buda BOOMP bum
Buda buda buda buda buda buda buda BUM

I hope it's not a big sacrilege if I get it wrong. But I said to him in a quiet voice—I was just a kid talking to these *jefes* and *capitanes*—and I said, "Danza del Sol."

And he said, *"¿Cómo, mi'jo?"* [What, son? Really?]

And I said, [yearningly] "Danza del Sol."

He turned to everybody, holding his maraca, this steel rattle with seeds inside; he had his big cape on, and the headdress with all the feathers. And he called, *"Sol!"* And so I led the Dance of the Sun. It's fucking crazy. . . . I led the dance of the sun, to these people who are keeping alive that tradition of the Aztecs. Ah, that experience. I felt very honored!

We went to the pyramids. We danced on the street, and a lot of people didn't wear *huaraches,* the leather sandals. Since I was a kid, I was able to take it, hopping on my little feet and jumping like a grasshopper.

One of the nights when the dance went three nights straight, I remember waking in the middle of the night. I saw the stone plaza filled with firelight or candlelight, and the dancers were going strong. The flamelight was flickering on their bodies and they were dancing the heartbeat. Drums are so powerful they can take you into altered states. The Dine use the drum to synchro-'nize their heartbeat. And so, some white anthropologists have "discovered" that it can take you into certain brainwaves. But the drumbeat can be a bridge to your other self. I woke and saw this stone place filled with flickering bodies and pounding drums. It was so beautiful.

I don't know if it was my mother's influence, but I loved fairy tales and stories of enchantment. Andrew Lang had a series of books like the *Yellow Book of Fairy Tales,* the *Red Book of Fairy Tales,* and I read them all. And I *loved* them. I especially loved the one about Sigurd and Fafnir. Sigurd killed the dragon.

I had a weird childhood, because it was enchanted in so many ways. I was enchanted by Mexico, by Scandinavia—by China and Japan. I had playmates like Sandro—I think he was half Swedish, half Italian. Jesse. My friend Greg was always down for adventure games. And Derek and I had both watched the movie called "Crow," and we wanted to live in a world like that. Every day we would go out into the playground and pretend we were people in the movie "Crow." We even had a special signal to announce to each other that we were ready to play the game. We'd pretend to draw an arrow. I used to go to his house in the mountains.

Longfellow was a decidedly more "white" school. A more privileged, more enriching education. In fourth grade I would draw ninja or Conan pictures for my friend Tomás. And he loved them. I think in exchange for my drawings I won his guardianship, 'cause he was the biggest guy in school. I remember a report card where my teacher said I was talented, but I wanted to spend all my time making drawings and eating apples.

It reminds me of this time as a little boy in 'Burque when it was night and there were orange lights, *luminarias* or lamps. There was a donkey or a small horse. I had an apple, and I gave it the apple and it ate it. I loved apples, and I used to throw out the cores wherever I could. Usually in my room, in the back of my bed. I don't know why it was so important to me that the cores be thrown nearby. There's something about rotten apple cores nearby me that I really liked. This was a habit that would keep up even into college. I remember a college roommate complaining that apple cores were thrown around.

Fifth grade was the year I became a freak. I used to do research projects on my own, and I became fascinated with China. At one point I wanted to be a Buddhist. It may have started with Teresa, Papi's compañera at the time. She was interested in healing arts, and she made us cut sugar out of our diet. It was the year after my parents separated and also the period when Mama was in a punk band. Anyway, I was taking this meditation thing seriously, and I didn't really know how to do it, but I tried.

I became interested in what I thought was Asia, especially Japanese history and literature. I wore Chinese girl shoes and sweat pants that were too small for me. Sometimes I would wear a red dot on my forehead. When everybody else was playing sports, I would go onto the middle of the playground and meditate. I started getting ostracized by guys that used to think I was cool.

My friend Greg was pretty much a champ from the moment he was born. He was a Richard-the-Lionheart type, all about honor, and a skilled martial artist. I sort of practiced them, too—used to be kind of an athletic boy. And throughout the whole year Nikko and I were best friends or alternately not, and then best friends again.

Meijie and Yuejie were Chinese sisters new to Albuquerque who didn't speak English very well. I befriended them and admired them. I liked the way they ran with stiff legs. I think they were going through a hard time. The Martineztown Community Center [after-school program] was an amazing adventureland, but I remember Yuejie sitting with her head between her legs, looking down. Meijie and I were like buddies, because we were the same age. I liked her forehead. Her eyes were shy. Once when I went to their house, we had dim sum. Another time we sat on the couch, gorged ourselves on sunflower seeds and watched kung fu movies for hours.

Mama was with Zhong, an acupuncturist, and maybe from him I got these sophisticated Chinese magazines. I would randomly steal characters and draw them onto my pictures, picking up Chinese legends from books. I remember this deity with a monkey head, in silken baggy clothes and strange shoes. I was into boy culture, ninjas and samurais, although I was also into dolls. They somehow coexisted. So I would draw warriors, demons and princesses and put Chinese characters on. Meijie and Yuejie came to my house, and they saw one of the drawings and started reading the characters out loud—Meijie could read most of them. They laughed hysterically. Apparently what I had written was nonsensical.

At the community center there was a bully. He was intimidating Miejie and Yuejie, and I stood up to him, although he was a lot bigger than me, and he body-slammed me.

Breakdance had come out. I was really into it and pretty good at pop-locking. Another boy was better—he could windmill. But I remember a lot of good tricks and moves. I used to carry around a cardboard and do it wherever I could find a spot.

One time my dad and I were driving to Barelas. I saw a group of kids breakdancing, so I wanted to get out and join. There was an older kid, and we were battling. He did this move where he put his hands into claws and scratched my face. Not hard, but it's a very humiliating gesture. And in response, I did a wave with my tongue. I could do a wave with my stomach, but I did it with my tongue. And before I took off I did a spin on my back. I was a fast spinner.

Another best friend was Yusuf. His family was from some-where on the East Coast, and they were Muslims. They had many kids—I think eventually about fourteen. At the time, the young-est was Zainab. My mom said that once when I was looking off into space, she asked what I was thinking of, and I said, "Zainab. She has such beautiful eyes."

She reminded me a lot of my sister Oraibi, who I was very proud of. I'll never forget how when Oraibi was born, I used to hold her in my arms and feel proud to have a little baby sister. When Karina was born her name was Oraibi, the name of a Hopi village. Cielito and I used to play a lot with Kari. She was very pretty but fierce. We used to tease her, because she was fun to tickle, since she was smaller than us, and she would start laughing. Then she would get upset, and she wanted to be left alone. "Stop, stop!" If we didn't, she would fight you. And her hair was really pretty, white as corn hair. Except for the back—this tangled little patch. I really love Kari a lot, you know? She's always very special to me, my little sister.

Cielo and I were closer in age and had a tomboyish relation-ship. Though sometimes, even early on, they would gang up and exercise girl power. And when I was playing boy games, I wouldn't let Cielo join in. She'd ask, "Can I please play with you guys?" And I would tell her to be a princess, and we would save her. That was totally unfair—Cielo would have been a very good member in the battle.

But sometimes Cielo was my protector. One time I was swing-ing on this little branch, and when it broke, I fell on my ass and got the wind knocked out of me. I looked up at Cielo and said, "Tell Mama that I'm dying!" And she just ran, you know—like a little brown lightning. She was going to go save me.

Kari was really tough. One time at my papi's when Nikko stayed over and we were telling stories late at night, Kari fell off the top bunk bed. She fell pretty hard, and she bent a metal chair. With her body. But she was fine. And another time she got a black eye at preschool from some boy, in a struggle about a wagon, and she punched him and gave him a bloody nose. *I wouldn't have messed with that.*

Albuquerque was fun to grow up in, because it was like a small town, and it was also multicultural. Many people around there think they're Hispanic, even though they're probably *genízaros,* detribalized Indians. But Spanish is often the language that's spoken, aside from the pueblos. A lot of the last names I grew up with were Archuleta, Archulete, Saavedra, Candelaria, Maldonado, and there were many people with the last name Baca. Spanish is a colonial language. There's probably only a few Spanish families, and others were actually *convertos.* Some were Jewish people hiding their identity. There's also Moors.

And my friends growing up, there's a crazy spread. I remember one kid I liked, a black kid whose dad was beating him. That made me really sad. He was a really cool dude. My mom made a stink about it, because she was working at the after-school program at Longfellow for a while.

There were some older guys, DJs and so on, at the Martineztown Center. A lot of them had a good heart, and they were nice to the younger kids. They weren't punks.

At eleven I started Washington. I was humbled by the idea of middle school, had been lackadaisical about school in the past, but I really worked hard. So I did well at school. That was the year that a lot of kids and one of our teachers came up with the idea to go to Space Camp in Alabama. It was a pretty bold move, and we actually ended up doing it.

Gifts of Desire and Respect

I'm driving at night again. Now I'm on I-40 East. To my left there are hills, and they're covered with a ghostly light. I want to talk about Joon Yee.

I met Joon Yee in November of 2000. I was living with my father, who was sick with cancer, and working at the Southwest Network. I went to visit some of my friends from college, my roommates from junior year, 'cause they were going to this football game between two East Coast schools, and we were from one of them. I was short on money—I had a job I enjoyed so much, but it wasn't very high-paying. I felt bad, because my dad was going to have a fundraiser [for himself] in Albuquerque, but I wanted to get a cheap ticket, and I found a good deal. He insisted that it wasn't that important for me to be there. I don't know. . . . I should have stayed maybe.

But I went to Nuri's house in New Haven, before I went to Boston. She and Oliver picked me up from the airport. I was really happy to see them, and I think they were happy to see me. I had been running with my father, like an hour a day, and had been eating really healthy, so I was thin and fit. I remember I was dressed in baggy jeans and had a blue beanie on. I had shaved off my moustache and beard. We went and ate, went back to Nuri's house and fell asleep.

The next day, when I woke, I went to say good morning to Nuri. I didn't have my contacts in yet. And I saw her roommate, Joon Yee. She had pale skin and long black hair, and was in sweat pants, very much herself just sitting there. She had her little space. And I—I put out my hand to shake it, because that was how I was used to doing things, with courtesy and kindness, how my parents both are. I think it weirded her out, or she didn't see me with my hand out towards her, and both she and Nuri laughed. I've always thought of how cultures and languages are connected to nationality and immigration, so I did a probably stupid thing and asked her where she was from. I didn't realize that many people from all over the U.S., whose parents' or grandparents' background is from another country, they often feel weirded out by that question.

So she was like, "I'm from New York." And I tried to rephrase it. Like what's your ethnic background.

160

"I'm Korean." And we danced around each other that way. I thought she was very attractive.

After I put in my contacts and came to the table and made oatmeal to eat, Joon Yee and I were playing around, comparing feet sizes, and my foot was twice as big as hers, literally. She said something about how growing up, she had known a lot of tall Latino basketball players. And thought they were cute. Then she did her Korean, practicing the characters. Not Hangul, they were the other kind.

I was used to doing things a certain way from living with my dad, and it was important to me not to impose on anybody. I wanted to make my food for the day and then go off and do things. So I made about a pound of oatmeal, and it turned out later it was Joon Yee's oatmeal. I didn't know, so I felt bad about that. It was oatmeal for women, extra calcium or something. But I used it all.

My idea of myself at that time was to be autonomous. I had gone through some hard experiences at Duke trying to redefine myself. Though there were *mejicanos* in Durham, the presence of Black folks was stronger. And Black music meant a lot to me, gave me courage and nourishment. When I was feeling down I would listen to Earth, Wind, and Fire. And when I was feeling angry, West Coast rappers. That was *I'm a strong person, and I know what my business is, I know where my place is and where I'm going. Might take you a minute to figure it out, but, you know, it doesn't really matter, 'cause shit . . . I'm strong.*

I also liked house music with a sort of spiritual singing, with messages of hope, strength and beauty. I didn't like the super-electronic stuff. I like things that are uplifting, so that music did a lot for me. Then when I was living with my father, I had lost so much weight from running, and eating differently, I became really thin. And toned. You could see all my muscles, veins—when friends hadn't seen me for a while, one said, "When I first met you, you were this super-masculine person. 'Cause you were so big, and you look very different. You had a lot of macho energy, and now you carry yourself differently, and your face looks so much smaller. Like you look little and cute." And he pinches his fingers together and goes, *"Little and-cute."* He meant it in a sincere way—this is how he perceived me. I think I wanted to be androgynous.

I was interested in avant-garde poetry. Things that were redefining what poetry could be. I liked visual poetry, a lot of concrete poetry. I liked Futurism because it was creative and explosive, although of course also fascist . . . at least Marinetti was. That's not cool. But I liked Dada. And poetry that experimented with form and was still very heartfelt. A lot of modernist art, and books edited by Jerome Rothenberg with others. Even more, Lucy Lippard's book *Mixed Blessings,* with all its ethnic art and women artists. What women and ethnic artists do with the legacy of modernism can be a lot more interesting than modernism itself.

And I had a lot of ideas about things I wanted to do, like arranging words into a shape, the way people like Apollinaire and Breton had done. So many shapes that I wanted to do. I also wanted to mix comic book art with poetry. I loved the Power Puff Girls—I kinda wanted to *be* a Power Puff Girl. And of course I love surrealism. Although not the macho and misogynistic things about it.

My vision was: bring to it a spirit of all the things I thought were beautiful about ethnic communities, including various Latino communities and the Black community and the various Native American and Asian communities. Bring an androgynous spirit of beauty, and also of heart and intense soul and expressiveness . . . pure heart, you know? So that would be the ongoing project, but this is where I was with it at that moment.

Those weren't things I talked about with anybody. Joon Yee didn't know about them, and we didn't know anything about each other. And that might've had something to do with our curiosity and obsession with each other, because we were mysterious to each other.

162

I went off to do my things for the day, and the next night I went and jumped rope—I was a very physical kind of person at that moment, doing a lot of exercise—and I saw a bunch of old friends. That night I came home to Nuri's house exhausted. I was lying on the couch. And I saw Joon Yee pass by. She was in this pink dress—it was more like a slip—and she had on flip-flops. She started playing the Mos Def CD that has "My Umi." I love that CD. That was another one that kept me alive in Durham. She had this kind of crazy, jumpy energy that was unique. And she put on a leather jacket to go to her seminar.

I was looking at her and kind of laughing, and our eyes met. I remember Joon Yee telling me later that when she saw me on the couch, she could feel my eyes on her. I thought it was interesting that she put a leather jacket over a pink slip and flip-flops in November and went out for a class that way.

I went with Nuri to the library. Later, we were all sitting at the table, when Joon Yee said, "I don't *like* girls, you know?"

I said, "What do you mean?" I don't remember exactly, but she said women's cattiness was something she didn't like or respect. At the time I was in a similar response to the macho-ness of men. She had quirkiness and strength. And a certain punkiness: *I don't have to do anything that I don't want to do.* And I was in her presence, so it made these things real.

Finally, the next day was going to be my last day there. I had to go to Boston to see friends I hadn't had a chance to see in so long. So before I went out for the evening, I said to Joon Yee that what I really wanted was to have a talk with her. I thought she was an amazing person, and I wanted to spend some time getting to know her. And would it—would that be okay? And she said yes.

I went out to visit Rick Chavolla. He was a dean when I was at school, one of my closest teachers. He was also like an uncle; that's why I call him Tío. We talked for a while, and he told me about things that he'd been going through. We talked about my father, who he had met a long while back. And he invited me to go with him to do something. He worked with the Chicana, Chicano and Native American students at Yale, and that night a circle was going to happen. When we got there, several Native guys showed up, and I met Wizi who was Lakota. He was just a great spirit and a great friend. And so were the other people there. We did a beautiful circle. It was a very special experience. I felt honored to be there.

The ceremony was private, but I can say that to start, we burned sage and another plant. These plants were meant to invite spirits to the circle. I've always felt a strong connection to plants. Sage has a gorgeous smoke and smell, very powerful. And we were going to have to banish any negative thoughts. No negative thought could enter into that sacred circle. Only positive feelings and positive thoughts, even towards our worst enemies. I remember asking myself, *Is it possible to feel only something positive even towards my worst enemies?* I considered the guy that abused me when I was younger to be definitely not on the friend list. And I thought, well, if it's possible, and in my heart I realized that yes, it was, it was happening. Only positive thoughts. We had created a sacred circle. If you can, imagine the smell of the sage and the presence of these beating hearts around you. And that was incredibly powerful, a sacred tradition, transporting. . . . I can smell it right now. Then we smoked the peace pipe. After the circle ended and we were walking away, I felt a good connection with all of the people who had been present.

I had this question in my heart about Joon Yee. . . . Should I try to make this into something? Is it okay to open my heart? How do I show this person how I feel? And is there a right way?

The sacred circle had taken longer than we expected. So I was running a little behind. But I had also said I would meet a good friend. He's mildly autistic, and we'd always had a special friendship. So he and I had dinner, and then I had to go.

I was late for Joon Yee, and when I got to the apartment I rang and nobody answered. It might have been eleven at night. I don't remember when I was going to meet her, but it might have been ten. Or ten-thirty. I waited and waited and kept ringing the buzzer, and I didn't know how to get ahold of Nuri or Joon Yee. I was getting worried. I think it passed over to twelve, maybe one! And I thought, *Maybe I'll just have to sit out here until morning comes, and maybe I can find someone to let me in then.* So I could get my things and continue with my trip. I waited inside the building, but eventually a person who lived there asked me to leave—he said he didn't feel comfortable with me waiting in the building. I tried to explain to him that it was okay, that I was a good person, but he was upset. He said, "Look, you know, I— you're going to have to leave. My father just died of cancer, and, uh . . . that's the last word."

And I said to him, "I'm sorry. My father is also dying of cancer. And I'm sorry to know you're going through a hard time, and you don't need to call the police. Is it all right with you if I wait in the lobby area?" There was an outer door and inner door, with a space between.

And he said, "Yeah, that's okay. I just don't want you inside the building." So I did that. Because he was threatening to call the police if I didn't leave. I kept trying and trying, ringing the doorbell. . . . I just thought maybe—maybe she's home.

And then finally there was an answer. I heard someone running down the stairs and it was her! She had woken up. And I remember being so happy, because I—I thought I had lost the time that I was going to have with her. Of all the things that made me sad when I thought I wasn't going to be able to get back inside, the saddest thing to me was I had met this wonderful person, and I wasn't going to be able to talk with her. But she came down and opened the door. So, then she let me in. And I apologized, and she apologized also because she had fallen asleep.

We just started talking. I told her a little about the sacred circle. And as we talked, I realized that she was shy, she was hiding from me. I was sitting across from her at the table in the kitchen, and she was playing with her hair and covering her face with her hair.

Somehow she started talking about how different women had been hitting on her, and she said that she—she would never want to kiss a girl. "I'm just—I'm just—a boy, you know?"

And I said, "Well, actually, you know, I'm just a girl." 'Cause that's how I felt. I was sharing about myself and about my sexuality and the way that *I* was. Then I realized there was an immense amount of erotic energy in the air. I think we were both wondering what to do with it. And I said to her that if she was a boy and I was a girl, then we could—we could kiss, and . . . that would mean that she had kissed a girl. And she laughed.

I said, "So, ah—can I kiss you?" And she said yes. We leaned across the table and kissed each other. And then she said, "We should go into my room." So we went, and it felt natural, and at the same time enchanted.

Our skin was very pale, reflecting the moonlight. We held each other and kissed. Somehow I could tell that neither of us had experienced anything quite like this. Ever. It was incredibly passionate. And I asked her if she wanted to make love, and she said yes. And so we did. We made love for a very long time, and we said each other's names, and we held each other very close. We looked into each other's eyes, touched each other's bodies. And we held each other's hair. And we slept for a while.

We were strangers to each other. Yet we were incredibly vulnerable, and there was something electrical and magical about it—and the way the moon was coming down over us. Her skin was so beautiful. It felt like moonwater. We wanted each other so badly. It was the freest and purest moment that I've ever had.

And in that moment we surrendered to each other, we gave something to each other. And we—neither of us knew what it meant.

Being loving to someone and showing through your behavior that you have admiration and love came easily to me . . . and not so easily to her. She had never had the experience of being that. It came naturally to me to make someone the number-one priority.

I think it had to do with my upbringing. And I quickly had the expectation that this was how the relationship was going to be.

We couldn't always articulate to each other what we wanted. We took it a day at a time, trying to feel each other across the phone. She worried that she had a deep darkness inside of her. She said that she was a very competent person who didn't know who she was. And there was this emptiness. But she didn't call it emptiness. She said it was an abyss, bigger than her, and the only thing that was real. I couldn't understand, but there was this feeling that she didn't know who she was. I felt very sad to hear that! And I comforted her. She respected me for being someone who knew who they were. And who had strength and confidence. At that moment I did. I was exercising every day and doing lots of things that were fulfilling for me, and the different parts of my life fit organically. I was spending a lot of time with my father, and we had a good relationship. I had a job, and I liked it, and I wasn't afraid of anything. I remember even telling her I wasn't afraid of nothingness. Because I had something that would carry me through. And she thanked me. She's a tough girl who's been through difficult things.

During wintertime my papi and I would run at least six miles. Every day. And sometimes Papi would cry when we were running, because there was tenderness in his heart. Hope, and a trembling longing for life. And every night before bed we would give each other a hug. There was warmth in the rooms that we slept in, glowing light. I slept comfortably every night. Nothing really troubled my heart. In the morning we would wake up at the same time and go running, and when we came back we would shower and he would put sesame oil on his skin. He said people from India did that. It gave his skin a beautiful glow.

I asked Joon Yee to come visit me for Christmas, and she did. I'll never forget when we saw each other in the airport. Ah, she was so beautiful. I was impressed with how light she packed—all she had was a little pink bag, black clothes and tennis shoes, and her journal. I only got a couple of days' break with her and then I had to go back to work. But the house was pretty big, and we were together a lot.

Papi definitely approved. He thought that she was a good person for me. Of course, he based this on the fact that she was very quiet and respectful, looked graceful and was slender. And very physically attractive. These are things that were important to him. Actually—temperamentally, they're probably very similar.

She also liked our cat that we called Estrellada, which basically means dazed and confused. When I went out to feed the dog—Cha-Cha, like "the gal"—she liked the affectionate way I talked to them. Like, "Hi, Cha-Chas! Well, he-LOHHHH! Haiee."

She started cracking up—"So funny how you talk to them."

One day she said sharply that she felt uncomfortable because I was being too nice. It made her feel like she couldn't be honest, and she couldn't be herself. And I was stunned. So I had to talk to her about some of my own darker emotions. In order to make her feel she could be herself. And I think I had to learn to not always be so gracious to her, because it put this expectation that I would receive the same thing; of course, that *is* what I *wanted*.

On her last day with me we went on a road trip. We passed Cuba and came to Jemez. We heard drums, so we went onto the reservation. There was an enormous dance going on, arranged so older and larger people were at one end. It graded down into the youth, even little children barely large enough to walk. Some people were doing the Eagle Dance and some were doing the Deer Dance. It was very beautiful, and the colors were radiant—blue and yellow and red and . . . I started to cry. Joon Yee said the colors reminded her of Korea.

And before we went to the car, we walked out to the peak that overlooks the reservation. A large hill or cliff. We stood there, and we didn't say anything. I think in my heart I was asking for the world's blessing. I faced the four directions and felt the wind. Then I realized that we had not asked permission to be there, and we should leave.

After she visited me, I didn't know what was going to happen. But I remember running the next day. I saw the sun and the cranes, the trees by the river, and I thought, *This will work itself out.* We continued to talk on the phone and write a lot of email. I had applied to Stanford, and I knew that I was going to be going there. That's also what my father wanted, and so I was going to move to California. Joon Yee and I decided to move there and live together. *We're going to do it! We're going to be The Ones for each other.*

The Fear and the Broken Sleep

I was going through a lot of stress. My money was tight, especially because I had another visit scheduled with Joon Yee in March. And the more I found out about Stanford, the more I realized the housing situation was a nightmare. Joon Yee wasn't excited about living on Stanford campus, so we decided to live in another city, San Francisco, Berkeley, or Oakland, or Daly City. But as I talked to people about housing in the Bay, I realized you have to put down a large deposit, and there's a lot of other issues. I also didn't know for certain if I was going to get into Stanford. I was anxious. Like, I'm going to have to move down there anyway, and we'll figure something out, get a job something like what I have now. Papi really wanted me to go to grad school. I never could fully imagine how grad school could be good for me, but he believed that it was the place for me.

When I talked with Papi about it, I said, "What if I'm supposed to be here with you?" And he just said, "Mi'jo, at the rate I'm going it looks like I'm going to be around for a long time." I wasn't getting much sleep. I was sick in bed when they called from Stanford and said I got in. *Oh, my God,* I was so happy.

Before Joon Yee came to New Mexico, I had also bought a car. I made a large down payment. My papi said, "You've got a new car and a wonderful girlfriend. And you got into Stanford. I'm very proud of you. Very happy for you."

I tried hard to get back into working out before the March visit. I couldn't sleep on the plane to New Haven, and I got there at night. I was so in love with Joon Yee. She played me music she liked, this group Drunken Tiger, rapping in Korean and in English. It was the most interesting and expressive music I had heard in so long. And I loved it. We made food together. She made Korean food, a *bugo gook* tofu, dried pollack fish and seaweed soup, and kimchi. She was very good at making her dishes. They had some of her grace and heart.

We were searching for each other, and we were clawing at the things that were separating us. There were misunderstandings and frustrations, and one or the other of us would be hurt. I had some fears—I worried some of them might be true. And although I wanted to share everything, there were some things I really didn't want to find out.

The night before I left was incredibly difficult for me. We wanted to synchronize our worlds, but there was also fighting.

After I came back from the visit, I was thinking a lot about the future and how I was going to make everything work. I had never done anything like this. Up to that point, I would smother stress in things that felt medicinal—solitude, reading, music, TV, movies. But the way I was living at that moment was hardcore. I was exercising every day and overtraining. And I wasn't sleeping well. I had broken sleep, and was often close to getting sick. My body was worn out. Around that time I started getting pains and tightness in my chest.

And I was haunted by a kind of relapse into memories from the years when I had been sodomized by my father's friend. It made me feel comatose or lost in a horrendous feeling. I had increasing anxiety: *What if those feelings keep coming back?* I had thought that I would never feel those things again.

I think it would have been better if I had followed my mom's and other people's advice and gotten counseling, but the counseling I had done never felt right. It took me deeper into the feelings. Is it better to forget, or to remember and work through it? But I was haunted. There were things I had never talked about with anybody.

I couldn't sleep, night after night, and I went into a crisis. So I went to the doctor, this family clinic, and I told him I had flashbacks of when I was sexually abused. And he was like, "I could give you medicine for anxiety, but you might get hooked on it."

I said I was really scared of feeling this terror again. "I'm afraid of fear."

And he said, "Look, I don't know what to tell you. I was in the Vietnam War, and I saw people go through things they could never get out of their minds."

I said, "But I'm sure there's a way I can get past this, right?"

He was like, "I can't say. I know of women that have been raped or abused and can't get it out of their minds."

Fucking great.

My father was sick with cancer, and I had these pains in my chest, a real tightness. My heart was hurting. I was exhausted, but I couldn't sleep—I was ragged. And I was afraid if Joon Yee knew how I was doing, she wouldn't love me anymore. It was a part of me that felt delicate. Like I wasn't in control of my own mind and my own spirit, and it was devastating. I felt freakish.

Before, I had felt self-reliant, free and happy, and then it shattered. I felt *What if I never come back to myself?* It went on for about three weeks, that extreme terror. When it happens for so long, it rips your consciousness apart.

I tried to get rest, but I then had a sensation of dizziness, as if my mind was emerging from my body and floating somewhere. I broke into a sweat and got very cold. A hair-raising feeling.

Later, I tried to explain it to another doctor. Whatever the criteria for becoming clinically psychotic, I had the sensation that the world was ending. My mind felt like it danced around trying to find a way to escape from this. And I couldn't. I wonder if that's how people feel when they're dying and don't want to die. What if that moment kept happening over and over and you could not ever escape from it? I can't imagine what it's like for people that have to deal with that kind of mental pain every day. People trapped in that for their entire life.

If it kept on for me, something would have to give. It was already buckling. It's the most horrible thing to be in this dark room and you're caught in the nightmare, but you can't wake up. Your nerves are on fire. They're being scraped by glass.

When I had spoken to my mother, she tried to put it in perspective. She said, "This has a lot to do with not sleeping," and she tried to help me calm down. So I tried. One day at work, I just said I was feeling sick and had to go home. I lay in my bed for hours and felt a little better. The attack had subsided. Then every day I would try to summon the courage and the strength to move ahead. I had to somehow manage. So much was at stake.

One night, all of a sudden Papi burst into the hall. He said, "¡Mi'jo!" I could tell something was very wrong. "Mi'jo, we have to go to the hospital. I'm stopped up." Earlier on, he'd had a catheter for a long time, but he had it taken out, because it was scraping the inside of his bladder, and it immobilized him in certain ways—he couldn't be active. I think for a long time he'd been having a lot of trouble urinating but was hiding it from me. And it had come to a head—he couldn't urinate any more. His bladder was completely filled, and he was in terrible pain.

I was trying to hold on. *You have to hold on for Joon Yee, for yourself, for Papi.*

172

Only There to Taste the Flower of Life

[Note: Itzolin did go to Stanford for graduate studies, and Joon Yee came with him. They lived together for several months, in a sunny San Francisco apartment, before the relationship ended. Then he rented a tiny, overheated unit in the same building.]

After Joon Yee and I broke up and Papi died, I went to Albuquerque with the family for his funeral. When I got there, I didn't have anything left inside of me. But at Papi's ceremony, his spirit and strength and his voice filled that space and filled everybody. When I came back, that's what was keeping me going, riding that light. I didn't have a lot of direction—I was just following this tide of energy. I went to classes and let life flow through me.

I was on some sort of weird high. I don't know if it had something to do with medicine, 'cause I was taking Paxil and Trazodone, and they made me a little sluggish and at one remove. This ocean-type feeling felt good. My pain flowed into comfort and well-being.

I went out with friends. Alfonso Gonzales and I had a kind of brother relationship that gave me strength. Other friends were Eric Manolito and Kuusela Hilo. Jenny Lam had an art project I would go to weekly that was very therapeutic.

And I would party a lot. It started out small at first, an every-now-and-then thing. But it felt really nice to have that warm radiance of friendship and laughter. I did a few poetry readings. Even though I had a broken will, life was carrying me upward. It was a very airy feeling. I didn't know why, but I felt intense happiness. At times there was intense pain, but it felt like something sacred was healing me. I think I cried about every day. I just let tears flow, sometimes tears of happiness, sometimes the tears of pain.

I didn't do any real management on my life. It was rough and tumble—wake up, get in my car, drive to school. Instead of planning things, the way I had done before, I would take things as they came. And I hardly did any schoolwork, a bare minimum. I almost didn't pass a few of my classes. I spent most of my time being with friends, staying up late with them, enjoying the times.

Sometimes I would read at open mike at Locus, a Korean cultural spoken-word thing or slam. That's where I met Ishle Yee Park, one of my favorite artists. And Annie Koh, who I had seen at school when I was an undergrad but never met. Jane Kim, Stanley Lam, and a whole bunch of people. Marilyn Yu, who worked at Galería de la Raza. Around that time I also started going to San Jose and met Melanie Palermo and other people doing women-in-hip-hop and women-of-color events, spoken word and DJ. My life was filled with art and spirit and culture and friends and parties. There was also a powwow at Stanford. All these things were converging in my life.

I felt really close to all my friends. I had elements of all these different cultures. Ultimately, I considered myself Chicano, but I felt a connection with my Native friends and a lot of Asian and Pacific Islander friends. I was high on art and life. Alfonso would say, "Are you on drugs? Are you high?" And I wasn't. Maybe the medicine contributed, but it was more the *texture* of my life.

When I went to school, I would stretch my poncho out on the grass and lie in the sun. Then go to classes, and at night hang out with friends. And drink a lot, smoke cigarettes, laugh and be free. There was this insuppressible laughter always inside of me. Though I still cried a lot about Joon Yee and about Papi—I remember times I would drive home from Stanford and tears would run down my face the whole time, thinking about how much I had lost.

I really liked drinking. It started off mellow at first and, when it got to be fun, more intense. I would go to an event where there were people I knew and drink a lot and talk. Sometimes I wouldn't get much sleep, yet I was able to function. I felt strong. Happy to be getting so much sun. I was leaning on things that were holding me up, but looking back on it, I wasn't carrying any of my weight. I felt spacy, alternately euphoric and mournful.

My strategy for dealing with deeper issues was laugh at my own pain. Sometimes I would talk about it to anyone who would listen, but I wasn't connected to it. I was not eating a lot of food, because I wasn't cooking or paying attention to my body. I got really thin. I could still do the twenty pull-ups and felt fine, but I wasn't. The feeling of happiness came at a price.

I would drive around by myself to different events and meet people, just go up and introduce myself and talk about things I was interested in. . . . None of that was negative. It's just that I was only there to taste the flower of life.

I met so many cool people, though. That's how I met Melanie. We immediately clicked as kindred spirits. She's a strong person who has her feet on the ground. Though I didn't. I was literally a wanderer, carrying around my poncho and my bag. And I wore turquoise earrings and turquoise necklaces that I had made.

I've always been the kind of person that has to work at balancing the concrete things in life. It takes me more effort than most people. There I was, thinking nothing can hurt me, but I was drinking so much, and I could. I would just sleep a little late the next day. I would get up, do some errands, and do it again. I felt like a carefree little boy. If your kind of radiance is reckless, it's probably not as sustainable as you think. It's like transparent flames were burning things up. There was a point where I realized *I think I'm not being a good person. Someone that just floats on life whose only real qualities are, you know, aerial grace and good muscles—what is that? Is that a friend? Is that a teacher? Is that someone that is actually offering something?*

People were starting to tell me about honoring commitments. But that realization didn't always matter to me. The sacrificial element of things was somehow intoxicating. Eventually it became a lot of unusual mental states. And then there was a period I was drinking so much I became disoriented. I had this desire to float, erase myself.

Ocean of Clashing Shapes

Then I had feelings of guilt. Because I wasn't really a good friend. I was meeting many people, especially women of color, that were active in raising awareness and fighting for a perspective on women's experience. And the systematic neglect of women's lives. Even though this was something I cared about and wanted to support, I wasn't doing anything to change things. I asked myself *What are you about?* And I didn't know. I was frightened that if I really came into contact with myself, I would see forces and impulses that were actually harmful. I could have maybe been more generous to myself. But I realized that there was a part of me that valued women more than men.

And really, if I thought about it, there was something potentially dangerous and hurtful in the male will. And male sexuality. I identified more with women. I wasn't invested in a lot of the things that I had been brought up to be invested in. I didn't want to impose my will on anybody or be macho. I didn't want to conquer anybody. A lot had to do with my sisters and friends. Because I felt like my sisters have been hurt by men. There are men that have done bad things to them and destructive things to their lives.

I was thinking, *In a lot of ways, men are the agents of a kind of hurtful power.* They're the ones who execute it. So I felt like in any situation, I would take the side of the women. If there was a conflict—not necessarily between men and women, but any crisis or problem demanding attention, I would trust women more than men. I had a lot of friendships with women based on respect, appreciation. I identified with a lot they had been through, even though it was probably impossible for me to imagine because, for physical reasons, I have always enjoyed male privilege. I'm tall and sort of stand out as this male figure, and something about all that makes me a man. But the things I was striving for and appreciated were things a lot of men don't understand. At the same time, I felt, *What if I'm actually dangerous because I'm a man?* A lot of men have been abused physically or traumatized by experiences or by their fathers or by situations, and it changes them. It makes them ugly.

In my relationship with Joon Yee, there was a reversal of roles. She was kind of the man, and I was kind of the woman. But what if part of me, by habit, perceives femininity as an object to be had or penetrated? And if I thought about what men wanted and what male sexuality was based on, in terms of roles I saw, it seemed like the woman just didn't count. As if the woman was there to please the man. Like the need for power had to be appeased. That's not what I want!

Many of my learned behaviors and repertory of thoughts and voices, even in art, came simply by having grown up in the role of a man for so many years. Even my father told me, "Just be a man." In my mind I would always laugh at that—"Oh, my God. 'Be a man.'" No! You know? Be a woman! How do you do *that?*

It bothered me that I didn't really know how to change things in an appropriate way. Something that's been so painful for me is to feel like you've hurt someone when you didn't mean to. When you interact with people, whether you like it or not, you enter into the making of group situations, group feelings and attitudes. And I thought *What if what you really are isn't what you hold inside but what you do for people and what you show?*

So if a community says, "You're fucked up," what do you do? Isn't that the point where your actions speak for themselves? But what if you're not good at managing all of the different opinions and evaluating what's right and wrong to do? And people lose respect or confidence in you? I could see many ways I wouldn't be good in a group situation, showing support through a long-term commitment, sustained actions. Because that's not so much who you think you are or what you know in your heart, it's how the group works. Piss off the right people, and suddenly you're not wanted any more. I've always had fear of people who have this power to make or break you. My worst nightmare has always been waking up one day to find that something I did unintentionally—or worse, out of a desire to do something positive—to find that it's completely alienated a group of people I cared about or wanted to be friends with. It's like getting *torn*.

Because I had started out early with trust and confidence in my world.

I like to show support by making a gesture and keep a distance. I don't really trust my social character. I'm not a very good manager of group mechanisms. I was feeling like I'll screw up, and then, in that situation, I will be the bad guy. When you're part of the community, you have to accept that people are going to call you on things and be willing to learn from it. But I'm not always able to respond to criticism well.

And I also felt like I couldn't be there for people in a real way, like my sisters. I had to learn how to try. It's hard for me to really be there for other people, because it's hard for me to be there for myself.

Some people, you can tell them, "Shape up!" And they know how they can. But I'm out of touch with the way that most people do things, and I like it that way. Sometimes I need to sleep a lot and I need to be alone. And if I don't get that sleep, then I'm subject to bad feelings.

There are also people I don't know how to empathize with. I'm usually able to tell what someone's emotional state is, but not always how they get there or what triggers or changes it. If several people are involved, it's a big guessing game. I saw how dynamic social situations were, that they tended to be created by people that were more outspoken, or had more of a presence, starting a group response. How do I respond appropriately, in a way that doesn't just make one person happy but that makes many people happy? Especially when not everybody agrees.

Drinking with people gave me the opportunity to see a lot of these things, 'cause I *wanted* to learn about the social world and how to be a part of it. But there was also that scary element, like "everybody's watching." You could alienate a bunch of people. And you're called upon to do quick thinking and take quick action.

I visualized someone who's good at it as being like someone good at playing the Japanese game Go. It has many different pieces, and the two players try to encircle each other's pieces with their pieces. And that's how they claim the opponent's pieces. People who excel at it, like child prodigies, are able to discern patterns through intuition—they just see the pattern instead of arriving at it through calculation. I realized that becoming an adult, in some ways, amounts to taking on some of this.

Some people have faith they can be who they are and everything will work out, but I don't feel that way. I don't like to make the mistake and get slapped and feel hated. But there are a lot of social situations where there really *is* no right answer.

Just because something is negative doesn't mean it doesn't also have the light of goodness, of beauty in it. I've always been good at avoiding things that make *me* feel bad. But . . . how am I going to know what's good or bad? All I know is that I feel love. And everything else is like an endless rolling ocean of things that clash and reshape and can be seen any number of ways.

It's possible to be surprised once you know more about a person and start to see the range of their feelings. Joon Yee and I turned out to be different and contradictory. The best of my love wasn't even what she needed. We couldn't be the right person for each other, and yet I loved her with all my heart. Learning to try to be the right person for her meant so much to me. Even though it was really hard and meant a great deal of sacrifice. And I know the same was true for her. I think a deep disappointment for both us was . . . *our souls don't really sing to each other.* And yet we really loved each other. Really needed each other. And just were crazy about each other. The contradictoriness and the desire to overcome it—that clashing of inability to really have our souls sing to each other—was also magnetic.

The things that hurt us—where do they come from? What are they? Are they really bad? What's true, you know? I can see things from different people's eyes. And there's something beautiful in that. Something beautiful I don't understand.

Bridges

Looking back, maybe I should have taken time off to recover. I wasn't showing a lot of care. Sometimes I would just eat brown rice or bread and bananas. Little bits all day.

But I'm grateful for all the connections I made with people. And I care so much about all my friends and my family. They're unique, beautiful people. Every single moment I spent with another person meant a lot to me.

Cherrie Moraga's classes became like another family—she's such a strong person. Fernando Birri was amazing. He reminded me of Papi. His joy in life and creative heart were uplifting.

Alfonso's a warrior but sensitive and perceptive. Linda is a special person. And Manolito is wonderful—he told me how, just standing next to a horse, he could feel its spirit. Kuusela has been a good friend and sister to me. Also Gabi. Her name is Erandi in Purépecha—she has a hummingbird spirit. Sometimes I can see her different journeys in her eyes. I remember Zamora and many, many people I respected and cared for.

Something interesting for me about Stanford was the way the Chicano Center, Native American and Asian centers are close to one another. And growing up in Albuquerque, there was a strong community of people from all different places, including a number of African-Americans. There was a feeling that everybody had this gift of their vision and cultural background. It was a leftist community, and everybody was artistic—so many rich things.

And although I had grown up in the Chicano Movement, I was fascinated by other cultures and heritages.

I went to San Jose for events where it was One Love, like a Floricanto. That word is from the Nahua *in xóchitl in cuicatl*, which means Flower and Song. I would see B-Girl crews and women DJs, so much heart and presence there. The vitality of different cultural backgrounds expressing themselves—Filipinas and Filipinos, Latinos and Latinas. I was also reading about the '60s and '70s, the time that was very formative for my parents, and learning about things that had happened. And the Bay Area, especially San Francisco. It was like everything was interconnected, and I would talk to people about them, especially with Kuusela. Like the I-Hotel movement and how beautiful that was. I heard Al Robles' poetry and saw artwork by Nancy Hom. The creative flow had included folk singers with songs in Spanish and Filipino grape workers who created momentum for the UFW. And when the Black Panthers went to China, they were respected as revolutionaries. I'd see people that were our elders and young people taking that on. I wanted to learn a lot of different languages—Nahuatl or Quiché, Tagalog and Mandarin.

The summer when Joon Yee and I had moved to San Francisco, I worked at a locksmith's where they spoke Cantonese. The boss was Hakka, from southeastern China. I was the only Latino in the place, and the ceilings were so low I almost had to kneel. That was a rough environment, but I learned a lot. I had to earn their respect. Everybody was expected to go out on a job with some lock that you don't even know how to do, and figure it out. You have a problem and you start solving it. If you make a mistake, someone tells you you're wrong and you fix it. Sometimes I'd feel helpless. The owner's wife, who spoke Mandarin, hadn't come into this with locksmith skills, either, but she was extremely effective, quick and ready. I wondered where she got so much mental stamina. The guys would cap on one young guy there who loved hip-hop, but I loved how he knew all these phrases in Caló.

My nickname at the time was Tito, but they didn't like it, so they called me Tilo. By the time I left that job, I felt like one of them.

I was also questioning *What does it mean to be Chicano?* And thinking about my own cultural background and roots. I was interested in my indigenous heritage and realized there were things I didn't know much about. My father's family, from a long time ago, might be Zacateco. And we also have a lot of Plains Indians, like Comanche. Also European influences, because of the Germans in Texas. And then my mother being Scandinavian and feeling a strong connection with the Saami, the reindeer folk.

I remember my mom told me something in early summer, when I described the cultural events and readings. She said, "I like the way you're finding creative things, because you're doing something beautiful with your pain."

And I think she was right, because I felt this bridge between all these different people, and it was like I was going to connect them. Especially through art. I've always wanted to do that. Like *These are the people I care about, and this is what they all share.*

Crazy Horse Rainbow

I've always had a desire to be different people. I *have* been different people. In college, I'd been thin my whole life, and I wanted to try something different. Within about a year I was a different person. I wanted to be big and strong, so I went from being slim to being this enormous powerhouse who weighed like two hundred and twenty-five pounds and was extremely strong. It was a very different feeling. Then a year later I decided I didn't like it. I wanted to try going back to how I was before. So I changed the way that I ate and made my exercise more cardio-vascular. When I went to live with Papi, I was doing all this running. I could jump rope for an hour—that was more anaerobic. I would go nuts and wouldn't stop, 'cause I was in that kind of shape. In winter, I'd do it outside, and I would sweat so much that I had to strip down to shorts in the dead of winter. So in another year, I was like a hundred and forty-five pounds and felt really different again. Some of my friends would say, "Why do you have to be so extreme?" But that's how I've always been.

One reservation I've had about school and the idea of becoming a college professor is that I don't feel a university captures enough from life. The things I have felt most are art and the people around me. The way they looked at things, the things that they shared. The things that they held back. People find their own ways to help or heal each other. I felt like I could be part of any group. I used to talk with Annie Koh late at night. I've also shared a vision of connecting different communities with Jane Kim, who does amazing things with them.

And music gives me enthusiasm. I've always loved *mejicano* music, especially conjunto in the Tex Mex style, 'cause I grew up on that. It reminds me of when I was a baby—love and happiness. Sometimes when I used to play corridos, I would sit there and make them up all day. I like Bach, Antonin Dvořak, Ralph Vaughan Williams, David Diamond, Ravel, medieval music. One time at Duke, Juan Carlos and I were thrashing to Beethoven. He turned me on to Héctor Lavoe, an incredible *salsero*. If I ever got the equipment, I wanted to mix hip-hop with traditional instruments, like *el requinto jarocho*, or one of those little *tres* Cuban guitars. One night, Stanley told me about a Japanese woman who could knock out drum and bass on regular skin, really hardcore, like Doom-doom-DAHT, doom DAHT, doom-doom-DAHT, doom-DAHT, a-doom-doom DAHT, doom DAHT . . . and it made me so happy to hear him talk about that. It reminded me of Azteca drums, when I was in Xinachtli.

In painting, I've always liked Picasso, Braque, and Miró. I like Jean-Michel Basquiat. He was almost doing poetry—mixing words with raw images. There's this phrase Artexto I picked up. I wanted to do stuff like that. I liked Wilfredo Lam a lot, a Chinese-Black Cubano who did paintings based on *Santería*.

In writing, I was always into Latin American poetry, especially when it was surreal and had new types of metaphors. Vicente Huidobro [Chilean poet] and César Vallejo [Peruvian poet]. I really liked Neruda. All that was like finding wild fruit in a forest. Books and writing have always been crucial for me.

The second time I dropped out of high school, when I came to live with my mom, I remember Ronnie Burk coming to the house—a family friend since I was born. I was worried, because I had so much love for him, and he was just scraping by. I saw how hard it was that he didn't have degrees. Here was this dude who had so much talent. And he just had it hard! I remember thinking, *Man. . . . I gotta do something*. Because my parents didn't have any money, and it wasn't like I was going to be all right if I didn't do something. Even though I was chilling with older writers who were really supportive, I didn't see how it was going to work out. What was I going to do, be a waiter for the rest of my life? I was scared. And I made a decision to pick myself up, do the impossible and go to college.

I worked so hard. I didn't have the best memory, especially in history class. There was something awkward about the way my mind works, so it was hard to streamline. I would read short stories, poetry and novels from all parts of the world and spend hours copying down lines. I found out later from my mom that my dad had done that, too.

I identified with a lyrical poetry tradition. I never really could figure out what poetry was. I don't relate to a lot of the North American poetic traditions. Joon Yee and I used to go to the library, and once she checked out some Korean poetry. She said, "I gotta warn you, they're very sorrowful poems." And I loved them. They were passionate, intense, and visual. It was like what my mom calls "modern-day Aztec thinking," where images and color combine to represent words. In Nahuatl, the word for a person was face-and-heart. Alfred Arteaga has riffed on *difra-*

184

sismo, that precolumbian hybrid of two words combining to bind two things—I always liked that kind of surprise. I feel Juan Felipe Herrera has done that a lot. My mom also. And Papi also.

The thing is that for every person accepted by an institute, thousands of people are doing amazing shit out on the street.

Just last week I went to APAture and saw a lot of old friends. Ishle sang a deep, heartfelt song in Korean that sounded ancient, and she read some poems, one of which she had written in Korean. It filled me with that limitless feeling. I felt dizzy, because I could feel what she was feeling, underneath this enormous sky and on a field.

I had kept saying I was going to have a birthday party and invite everyone. And I should have done it, you know? It would have been a wonderful festival. But by the time it was time, I had already been through a lot. There were two big presences, two rays piercing me, Papi and Joon Yee. I was kind of losing myself. And I felt I wanted to protect the people I care about, not expose them to that wild, flinging-myself-out-of-my-own-feet feeling, not be a burden. Although trying to be a tough person was a mistake. I should have cared for myself.

I shared so much with these wonderful people, and it was like the purest heart of me was able to be with them. I always felt like my real nature was exuberance, that feeling that life was enchanted. And then maybe there's also something dangerous. The pain was so intense. Maybe it drove my spirit out of my body.

I wonder what really happens during the Sun Ceremony. There's a crazy horse inside of me . . . a rainbow.

Powerful things resonate in me from living in New Mexico and growing up there. The silence and the way that the elements move. Rock and wind, the sun and animals. And growing up by the Rio Grande. You feel presences like the cranes. The coyotes and roadrunners. And the snakes. Smells of the earth, like sage. Stones, the precious stones. The way that the sky surrounds you and fills you with different colors. And the sun. There's no sun like the Southwest.

A lot of people have been through things like I've been through, and some of them are probably more like me than I am. They have this craziness *que los impulsa* [that propels them], you know? And I admire them. In San Francisco you meet really talented people who live on the edge. I don't want anything bad to happen to them—I hope they have a lot more balance than I do. Some of them have even been down the drug road, which I never did. But they can still get up the next day and just do their job. And that's more than I can say, you know? That's one of the things that has fallen away.

I think I was lucky. My mother, my sisters, who I love so much. In a lot of ways I think that my mother is the most beautiful person I know. And I believe that I inherited from her this kind of passion and love for things in life that have to do with the heart, and that vision of things interconnecting. I really believe that life is a flower, that everything flows out. Radiantly.

And the flower is the heart. The heart is the universe. Sometimes you can see how all that connects to the other lights in the world. The earth and plants, and in other lives and in the sky. I've never been afraid to explore those things.

And I believe that everyone is born innocent. That in a sense, everyone is innocent. The way I grew up, certain things like *cariños* [signs of tenderness and affection] are so important. *Hay que hecharle cariños a la persona que amas, ¿no?* [You've got to give affection to the person you love, right?] *Mahal kita. Saranghae. Wo ai ni.* ["I love you" in Tagalog, Korean, and Mandarin.] Those are very important things, you know? *Te amo.* When I feel people's energy, it's like a *bendición* [blessing]. Or even a *milagro* [miracle].

I'm still that kid that did the sun dance in Mexico City.

There's a lot of beautiful ruins in my past that I don't even know what they mean, because there aren't that many people that are there to affirm their meaning for me. If there is such a thing as a witness, it's the earth. And we're just children or visitors.

186

Some of my struggles have been beautiful. My struggle for Papi and Joon Yee was beautiful. And my family and friends now are gorgeous. My mami and my sisters and the rest of the family. My older brother, my two older sisters. I have so much love for them.

I have a lot to thank for all the creative hearts I've connected with.

There are many people that I'm leaving out. I hope that, if I am not able to remember all of my friends, they'll still remember how much they meant to me.

I was very blessed to be around so many beautiful spirits. And I wish that fire in me would always burn.

Can something burn always?

Itzolin, thank you for showing me your heart and sharing your love for music and for the people and the community with me and so many of us at Stanford. Thank you for showing me the beautiful land that you called home. I always remember your heart of fire, my dear friend.

—Kuusela Hilo

I met Itzolin, while in college and far from my homelands of New Mexico. I think our first encounter was at the local El Centro Chicano student center. A few times during the year I'm reminded of Itzolin. The start of the Fall season, I can hear him talking about trips to the beach and there sharing stories of New Mexico. We would drive out in the evenings, along with other students and enjoy the beaches at night. During the Mother's Day weekends, I remember the Stanford Powwow events and us walking around the event. Much laughing, eating and visiting.

From a poem I wrote years ago, "Smell the ocean air we danced over on those familiar months that play over and over . . . play a guitar with me once more, play over a Patrón bottle once more." The poem is called "Draw Another Baca Girl with me Holmes" and it relates to our experiences of New Mexico and always having a friend with the last name Baca. Since those college experiences, I remember Itzolin a few times a year. With new creative writing, Itzolin is a character in a "long story" still being developed.

—Eric Manolito

Sugar skulls made for Día de Los Muertos

I was blessed to be in two Kearny Street Workshops with Itzolin. While teaching "at-risk" teenagers at an alternative ed. high school I read them some of his poetry and showed them his art. They were inspired and thought his artwork was "tight." When we shared Día de los Muertos with our students, they really dove into this loving place. We made an altar, remembered loved ones, made sugar skulls, papel picado, and paper flowers; and we made bread, hot chocolate, and danced. I put Itzolin's picture on our altar with others. He had this light, and he has a permanent place in my heart. Despite the hard loss, I take inspiration from Itzo's strong vision of artistic community.

—Kim Mizuhara

Itzo would say that he wanted to live as poets live, in the moment. He would refer to them as those "crazy cats," Juan Felipe Herrera, Al Robles. They embodied what Itzo saw as the poet's essence. What I wanted to say to him was that he need not look further than the image of his own reflection to find a true poet. I don't need to give you examples of his intelligence, kindness, compassion or humility. It is the sum of these gifts that make Itzolin a poet at heart and in life.

Itzolin will always be with me. He drove me home from class for the duration of eight brief rides, and at that time it feels as though we crossed borders and bridges and boundaries to see one another, I mean truly see. This is rare to have and I wish that for everyone.

—Truong Tran

2003 Self portrait in his apartment, the Mission, San Francisco

Note on a scrap of paper:

Everybody has some sort of crush on causality. "Oh, now how did this get here . . . ?" That's not interesting to me. What's interesting is what it actually is. Consciousness *is* what it *is*. Like the transparent crystal, kernite. I hate process. Everything is just a bunch of destinations. A life isn't better because "I did great things." It's just work. I'm interested in new. It's why I like stories—take an old thing and make a new thing. After you read it, that makes a new thing in the world.

—Itzolin Valdemar García

PHOENIX HOTEL

POEMS

ITZOLIN VALDEMAR GARCÍA

Para Papi

Coyotes

run on

the scalp of the desert . . . the black whispers

laugh three voices   home is your bed

begin where you are born

fly like nails of fur   other places   newborn

return and cry

water friend like water

the wind changing the leaves in the sunlight

     that is coyote

         Gota Roja . . . ya naciste   mi'jo mestizo

      Red Drop . . . now you are born

          my son of mixed blood

Coyotes   catch mirrors with their eyes

              steal words in the canyon

        Spanish names   Nahuatl songs

              bonfires of Chinese sounds

              born born each second

Codex Itzolin

Book of red eyes
Of black hands

Zacateco eyes hold the corn   they tear away the leaves
inside is a baby   his skin is red   his tongue is a gold moth

The young Xicanito always wants to walk without clothes   his
body hurts him   one day he begins to scratch at it and he finds
green and blue feathers beneath his skin   scared, thirsty,
wanting to touch the sky, he strips off his outer layer   he lifts
the trees of his arms   his friends help him to move
he no longer has a sex
he has memories   his feathers are made of old voices
the colors bend from his arms and touch the world

Mira nomás   see that bird   his eyes always looking at you
his turquoise blood

What do you see behind closed eyes?
the white sky crossed by the jaguar of ink?
the woman whose hands make a bowl filled with red circles?
the mountain that pushes until it makes light into stone?

You, have you always known you are a jaguar? a jaguar made of
the night

Paint what you see
all the hands   all the eyes

Hardcore {conga^anger^SUNversion}

There was a conguero from the barrio of Oxenqui   they called
him Tres because he could play as if he had three hands
instead of two   he played bongo   kettledrum   congas
sometimes the drums cried like a water of eyelashes
sometimes they pounded the forest like parrots splintering the sun
even when he spoke, his voice poured with clouds and whispers
crocodile skin   sleep and rain
shells rubbed through a dark embrace
booms of love   untuned wood
BAN ban bTA-GA-**GAN**

Tres came to the big city from the island   he needed hard cash
he thought he could play his congas for money   at first it was
good   he smiled when he played   he was nervous his hands were
like wooden children   like four or five island parrots   clapping
feathers   bamboo lightning   he let loose wherever the congas
took him   he played from deep in his arms   rRRRRapid stuTTers
sometimes when a nice person walked by he would do a different
sound   the sound of a saint breathing   a fish drinking leaves of
sun   sugarcane sweating blue frogs   he worked underneath the
little streetlamp   <he leafed and streetlamped the music>   the
wet shadows moved around him and did yoruba prayers   he took
off his shirt and his eyes wrinkled in devotion
but after days and days and days Tres was damn tired   there was
no money   the sun was getting dirty   his shirt was lost   he hadn't
eaten   his eyes were red   no one listened to his congas   no one
no one   when someone looked into his eyes it was like +dirty
punk+   +bum+   +hustler+
Tres was becoming angry   something was wrong   he knew he
deserved to live
some young boys from the barrio noticed him   but Tres didn't

198

want to be noticed by them   they had mean eyes   they talked
dirty like beaten dogs   like roosters that fight in the pit   like
prison men   but Tres had a heart that pumped fire   he wasn't
afraid   he wanted life even if it WAS mean
So they finally came over to Tres and they started to mess with
him   they made fun of his congas   they called him an old bum
they told him to go home   they called him grandma and said they
were going to hurt him and no spirit was going to save him

      Tres wasn't afraid   he said they would learn one day,
        yeah, one day they would learn   he didn't care
    THEN ONE OF THEM TOOK ONE OF HIS DRUMS AND
              STARTED TO BREAK IT
   BREAK IT ON THE SIDEWALK   INTO PIECES   INTO DUST
something happened to Tres ***ANGER*** his beat changed   he
cackled it   staggerSLAP   smashing light between the seeds of
maracas   a roar   swallowing rocks   foam between clacking
   trunks   splashing candles   inside of Tres   he was rattling
           />rapping wood and
       shadow   { *savage*TIDE *fast* }
with such hollow SPIRAL growls   that they   that something
opened up the sky and fell down like a black war of tears   like a
      band of Taino victories   a passage of light
something passed through all of them   their palms groaned   their
        eyes rolled back into their heads
   masked animals filled their skin their heads   their arms
  they felt ANGRY LOVE SUN POWERS   the moon skidding
    the howl volumed through a thousand turning shells
Tres and the boys jammed HARDCORE   they gave their whole
bodies to the dance because they felt it   they felt it
the clouds were with them   they played hardcore
they jammed like this for hours or maybe it was days   their
wildness grew but so did the SONG   so did the congaBLESSING
they felt wood burning deep inside of their bodies   trembling

they threw themselves into their skyHALF
they couldn't stop   they felt a spiral of water   a candle of
shadow giving off spines   golden eyes   they felt echoes in tree
trunks 100 feet high   they felt smooth shells turning and turning
inside the moon

      they felt tusks and elephant skin across their foreheads
            they felt hot waves drinking
               their anger and
          throwing them far against rocks
            they were sucked back
           they were thrown again deep
        into the sky   far into the street
              into the city
         the smells of rice and bananas
            speedHANDS

        the boys woke up from their dance
        they woke up and felt weak from
     MACHETE winds   they weren't angry anymore
          they weren't angry at all
   they were thirsty and wanted to go to their mothers
         they all looked at TRES   he was
covered with the night   his loud pulse his strong breath
       TRES clapped his hands together
    their black surfaces   one loud cry to another
        his hands became   WIND
          ^ THROWING ^
            FIRE
     his hands were his congas   his
       hands were his congas

Járcor {conga^ira^versiónSOL}

Hubo un conguero del barrio de Oxenqui
le llamaron Tres porque tocaba como si tuviera tres manos
en vez de dos
tocaba el timbal   el bongo   las congas >
a veces sonaban como un agua de pestañas
a veces golpeaban el bosque como papagayos astillando el sol
aún cuando hablaba su voz se derramaba con
nubes y susurros   pellejo de cocodrilo   descanso y lluvia
conchas frotadas entre un abrazo
oscuro   estampidos de amor   madera desafinada
BAN ban bTA-GA-GAN
Tres llegó a la gran ciudad desde la isla   ne'sitaba plata
pensaba que con las congas le trajeran $ al empezar le iba bien
sonreía cuando tocaba   traía nervios   sus manos eran como
niños de madera   como cuatro o cinco papagayos de la isla
palmeando alas   relámpagos bamboo   tartamudeos rRRRápidos
le encantaba descargarse   y pensó que a la gente también le
gustaría   tocaba desde lo hondo de sus brazos   marchas y
plenas golpes suaves   tartamudeos bajos   a veces cuando pasaba
una persona buena le hacía otro sonido   el sonido de un santo
respirando   un pez bebiendo hojas de sol   la caña de azucar
sudando ranas azules   trabajaba debajo del farolito   las sombras
mojadas se movían alrededor de él y hacían rezos yorubas
se quitaba la camisa y sus ojos se arrugaban con devoción
su garganta hinchada   sus dientes fuertes abriéndose
pero después de días y días Tres estaba cansado pa'l carajo
no había dinero   no había plata   el sol se estaba ensuciando
se había perdido la camisa   hacía demasiado que no comía
nadie le escuchaba las congas

nadie pero nadie nadie   cuando alguien le miraba a los ojos era
como pa' decir   +vago+   +basura+   +hijueputa+
pobre Tres   se estaba enojando   sabía que
algo estaba mal   sabía que se merecía vivir
pues pa'ese momento lo vieron unos muchachos del barrio   pero
no era bueno   Tres no quería que lo vieran   tenían los ojos
cabrones   hablaban mal   como perros golpeados   como los
gallos que pelean en el reñidero   como hombres de la prisión
algo tenía que pasar   pero Tres tenía un corazón que tamboreaba
lumbre   no tenía nada de miedo
quería la vida tan siquiera si estaba cabrona
pues por fin se tiraron pa' Tres y lo empezaron a amenazar
se burlaron de sus congas   le llamaron un jíbaro viejo y le dijeron
que se caminara pa' su casa   le llamaron agüelita y le dijeron que
le iban a meter un puño y ningún espíritu lo iba a salvar
no le dió miedo a Tres   él dijo que algún día aprenderían
jei   algún día aprenderían   no le importó
ENTONCES UNO DE ELLOS COGIÓ UNO DE SUS
TAMBORES Y LO EMPEZÓ A ROMPER   'MANO
LO EMPEZÓ A ROMPER AHÍ EN LA CALLE   LO
HIZO PEDAZOS   POLVO
Tres se volvió loco   cogió otro de sus tambores y lo estrelló en la
calle   ¿ASÍ? gritó   ¡JEI!   ¿ASÍ?   los muchachos se echaron a
reír y empezaron a romper todos los tambores   cada cual estaba
rompiendo cosas   hubo VIOLENCIA
pero entonces algo se rompió dentro de cada uno de ellos, los
muchachos, dentro de Tres   algo abrió el cielo y se cayó como
una guerra negra de lágrimas   como una tribu de relámpagos
como un viento sagrado   como un lamento de frutas cazadas
algo pasó por todos ellos   todos se enloquecieron   sus ojos
rodaron pa'trás en sus cabezas   animales enmascarados les

llenaron la piel   las cabezas   los brazos   sintieron **AMOR**
ENOJADO
SOL POTENCIAS
toda la calle chorreaba gritos
Tres y los muchachos siguieron rompiendo los tambores pero
fue un ritmo   fue una canción vieja que ni siquiera sabían tocar
nomás le tiraron   le dieron sus cuerpos enteros al baile   porque
lo sintieron   lo sintieron   tocaron járcor
así se descargaron por horas o quizás días   su ira se creció pero
también la **CANCIÓN**   también la **BENDICIÓN**conga
sintieron una madera que se quemaba en el fondo de sus cuerpos
sintieron una espiral de agua
una candela de sombra soltando espinas   ojos dorados
Sintieron ecos en troncos de árbol cien pies de alto   sintieron
conchas lisas que giraban y giraban dentro de la luna   sintieron
dientes y pellejo de elefante sobre sus frentes
sintieron olas calientes que bebieron su ira y los arrojaron lejos
sobre unas rocas   que los chuparon hacia atrás   que los echaron
otra vez pa' lo hondo del cielo   lejos pa' la calle   los olores a
arroz y plátanos   los sonidos de auto   los negocios de la calle
los muchachos se despertaron de su baile   se despertaron y se
sintieron débiles
ya no estaban enojados   ya no estaban enojados para nada
tenían sed y querían volver a sus mamis
le miraron a **TRES**   estaba cubierto de la noche   de la
humedad de aliento de espíritu
el farolito hacía una corona de rostros sobre su pecho
su latido bravo
su respirar fuerte   **TRES** no se paró   **NO   NO**
todavía estaba tocando
ya no tenía congas pero no le importaba

nomas batió sus palmas   las superficies negras

un grito fuerte contra otro   sus manos se hicieron dos orishas de

madera   tocó más y más fuerte

lloró con todo su corazón

VIENTO TIRANDO FUEGO

sus manos eran sus congas

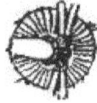

       sus manos eran sus congas

The Place My Mother Writes From

A planet filled with glowing fish, abandoned pillars, breath of asteroids, living moving clouds that speak. The planet's overpowering ocean and its purple afternoon skies. Messages she sends her friends in flashing smoke. To see her loved ones, she must spin out ladders of damask and cornsilk, ladders that cross space and memory. People find a way to cross. They speak with her for days about the huge fjord of space. Her fine lunar shells, space whales beached on icy stones, the birds of yellow fire that only sang notes from a scale no one had heard. She said with her smile, *Take what you truly need, my child.* At the top of the mountains, see her open arched hands, with lilac veins, with the softness of water reflecting life, with all the pains of mystery and loss held quiet. For this moment, the sky, for love of her hands, folds and moves and lights itself stretched over her fingers, like a beautiful headdress for a newborn girl.

Food Memory

We must eat
The world slows toward the sunstar
The sky wets the rocks   the ships
of ice soon will scrape the peaks of sleep
We must eat
The wind soon will fold ash in the
mountains and the blue eyes
We must eat
The cliffs soon will sing milkfingers
Over the stonewater   the greenface
the silver earth
Soon the hanging sky will quiet
the hour's red pain
Steam will cloud the nostrils
of the reindeer
We must eat
The fish soon will climb the lastrays
to the head of the glaciers in the sky
We must eat bread and fish
We must open the fjordskin
We must hold the shaking hooves
and drink the starmilk
Under our ankles the fire
turns the earth's mouthtime
The fourwinds rustle evening
with the voice of their feathers
We must eat

We have ironsongs and
pewter in our green fingers
We must eat
Tomorrow to steamdance
To open the skyfloor with reindeer hooves
To smoke the wind's moss
To bone the light of water

Tlazolteotl Breakdance

What is a b-girl?
The moon is an album
time to spin   my dance with yours
The laughter of the zoquete
The music is a staircase of red sand
The yellow flowers spark the rain
The black clouds cry mirror children
The pine trees tremble their crystals and touch the albums
my motion with yours
the sun's eyelashes surround the breakdance
My dance
    Break
        Your dance
            Tears of dawnlight

What is a b-girl?
    Rainbows in my feet
        The sky drums in my arms
            Movement
            33RPM
          What is a b-girl?
              Bamboo fluttering
                  Above the earth

Ermilia Graffiti Rose

Ermilia   you leave your photos your purse accidentally on the
bus   the city picks them up and takes them   grandmother cries
your name and ties her silver hair around you   but the city takes
your purse   your photos
The city pictures you   **BRIGHT**   it throws an album of your
face   your body   on the bricks   fast   a silent altar a ghetto
rollercoaster   your face on the wall of the cathedral   the bad

city watches you as you dress yourself
with hairspray every day   the slang of
sounds that runs across your cheeks
your armpits   the mural of your
footsteps   going down the avenues
the bakeries on Mission Street
your family hiding in the paint on the
walls   their eyes white behind the broken crazy words   the
city wants you to belong to it   wants your face to cover the
high tenements like a shadow   dark paint   but every night you
escape again   the moon slipping over your eyelids   over the
bread onto your mother's forehead   the frame of her hands
your little brother sings street rhymes in the morning   rap suns
his brown voice flying above the table   mariachi saxophones in
his plate of rice beans
The bus is where you talk   the whispering doors the
sleepwalking voices   spraypainted in your ears   on the windows
your friends tell you that your lips are a mexican movie   your
mouth opens   your laugh rises in black script   your body a
moving canvas of night and sex   there is a nocturnal rose
between your legs   your homeboy your boyfriend embraces you
his words are bruises falling on your back   he gets your bra

210

he sweats glassbeads and blue roses   you lie back   your hair
spreads in maya sounds over the bed over the radio   its sharp
voices full of burning corners   beating highways   your skin
opens in a theater of light notes
Discosatin   wet wheels   you cruise smooth in the car
light twists behind you   bending your face on the dented water
of the car   you are with your homegirls   in their room
watching the tv   your skin is the screen   you shine with flashes
masks   words   your small heart stretched like water
I fucken hate school   no way
I ain't with Arturo no more I
wanna get messed up tonight
but it ain't like that   the tattoo of your voice spreads in the
room with blue roses   surfaces of ink   you see your name in
your friends' eyes
Ermilia   your family love   your baggy pants   the drawing of
two clowns that you made on a *paño*   smile now   cry later   one
clown cries drops of sky   rivers of injury   the other's teeth open
with movie theater smiles   you remember the jail where they
held you for a night   they held your hunger your throat full of
penitentiary moons   spray paint   full of birds   birds   you want
a car   blurred metal   speed of voices   a blue murmur
Ermilia   your lips of black sun   your skin of wet caló   mute
lights   behind you stands your grandmother   her soft fingers
she places your hand in your boyfriend's and seals them with a
thousand stitches of sun   the two hands covered with crosses
with red beads
Your little brother misses you when he tries to fall asleep
without you   hears the echoing call: *Ermilia. ¿Estás, mi nieta?*
Ermilia, are you there my granddaughter?   Are you there?   Have
you let the city paint the hallways of the tenements the oiled
pistols of the eyes   turn you into a wall of laughter   sadness?

And when you are gone   who will search for your laugh? Who
will touch your eyelids? Who will know your voice of
pure graffiti?
Ermilia is in the car   the city scratches at the windows
Ermilia looks at the masks outside and laughs   she finishes her
cigarillo and throws the *colita* out the window:
Those pictures, you can have them. I never liked them anyways.
That just ain't me, ¿me entiendes?

To Know Your Place

it's nice to finish a day of work   come home
and eat oranges with my father
a colgar los guantes, mi'jo, y echar relajo
let's hang up the gloves, son, and relax
i know you have to get your hands dirty   struggle
it's good to know your place
you have done well

in grad school i moved backwards
fingers growing long to trap information
mouths opening
to let machines emerge   metal parts clanking

when you are hiding in water
you breathe through a reed
so i took my father's extra catheter
the thin plastic tube
no one noticed it snaking out the window
i hid the other end in my sleeve
i pressed it to my lips
and pretended to be thinking really hard

when i flew out the window
an old filipino man gathered my pieces
he liked the words
the way they looked next to each other

he showed it to his friends

Martín

My name is Martín Zambari
My shirt will explain it better   my shirt which is the evening
unhanded by the horizon to my feet, my limbs
Look at my shoes   they are the unusual kind   whose making is
like a clay bird or guitar peg
And we speak of the crude manufactures of old countries   which
you will not remember and I will not name
The ships and voices of that horizon are my belt   my kerchief is
a white map blank with tears and the smell of electrical wires
Will my hands explain it?
My moustache is a crisp bird   a snapping violin   an aboriginal
angle of fire or burnt salt
It will explain to you
My preoccupation with time, with death   who is my uneasy
friend   with the steel form of feelings
I will not tell you about my sisters, my mother or father
my retreating home
For the longest time I have been feeble   caulked in my limbs
with the hardening stillness of age   with a surface of moons
I have in my hair a cloth of humidity
I have a butterfly smoked and tied to my face by appearance
it moves my lungs into the single cloud of a clothed saint
masked with pieces of mirror and teeth of matches
Clavos, nails have repaired my heels   my accordion eyes
May I show you my death?   because he is watching me   he has
given me a message
He gave me a ring of dull silver   it is water, it directs my cough,
my breathing blood
Do you know where I keep what I have eaten?

It is kept in my throat
A fibrous tissue of sounds with my bones at their center
a transmission on wires,
my crackle to my mother   and the woman who held my chest
in the middle days of my labor
And my voiceless son
who had the needle heart and stone hair
who writes this with his illiterate fingers
Although I hold an orange in my hand
it forces itself against my insides
My nodes are of rubber, my pupils grommeted
I have investitures of silence   and the citizenship of matted
roots
I watch what you will not   the smell of blue flashes in windows
the firm bale of life wrapped
the rain compressing its origins on the crooked roofs
I know the road smell of fishes   alkali
tumbled better than paper
The startled journey of the grass
The wind's shifts of knives   the surge of fences
I have a patient lung
My breath is opaque with leaves of *cacauna*
My smile is a sketch   regret and the tears of a pierced grape
My home—it fills me   a harp of blurred street lamps
Of bent vowels, trampling:
Cross my hands
And forgive my thirst
For among my few sights I see
The corner in which you pass by and I pass by and the air rings
with gold macaws

Little Girl Who Has Bicycled a Painting

your ribbon of bluebrushes

the vault of

twosights   twoeyes

two final birds
which repeat
your heartsketch   which sing
real

hair ker chief

your ear of
distancefright

your ear of
oxygensound

your chirping toothache

of red easels
skystage
the saintbaths
where the bluelength retires
the sleep of the eyes
where the sailors in the hair
gather the fumes of the
blindharbor

your   **above**

your sunset cheek

the soft
tissue where
all you smell you
lacetouch on the gallery of echoes

your braid

your spiralbulb
where you eat the sky
the sum of
tragic shapes

left
your tradehand
where you save the
port of clefs
the musician's journey
the clouds' daughter on
stilts disappearing
with victrola crowns
heartlips
the chair of
your love's river

your sounds of

your braid of

right
your honesthand
the immortalafternoon
the outdoorclothespin
the horizon and blueking
of your fingernails
the shape of the rain
in your marks your
palmballet
the furious sunveil
that will blow
change to your
exact fingers

center

moon arcades

torsogame
medieval olivecolor
mass and sky
the belly which
has the pigeonband of the oceanhall
the almanac of space
you ride
you oftenwheel the summeryear
fly to the laterwoman

reflectedwater
run to the scene
where you pommelbalance
the banquet of twilight
the seas of lead
the murals of laughter
the walk for hours

below

the shorthemmed earth   the doorknobs of the knees
your legs which ruffle cartoons   where the touristwheel kisses your shoes
the crowd in the fireworkshrub   you knock over the clayfather
the vineyard of tinlaughter   where is your overnoon?
    where is your oceanjacket?   your mask of rainflowers
        where is your old face of time?

Barrio Comix X Series 99

You are reading the comics as you get a ride to school   to the
gangster playground, the walls covered with **VARRIO PUEBLOS
Y QUÉ ?**   you read, you look into the comic face   the frame
swings around you   your face and organs are copied
studioflashed, traced   first you are a glass motion, an idea, an
echo on the lips   then someone draws you   the frame begins to
tighten around you   your eyes awaken they are no longer filled
with sleep   you are a motion of **INK**, a **STENCIL**cloud, an
evolution of destroyed cubes in space   you are now **SERIES 99**,
a **COMIKBOOK** figure   you run through the parlors of ozone in
the high school   through the windows of sun in **CLASS**   Your
face is **XEROX**flashed   cut copied 1000 x, spread through
groaning hands   your body is a melting cadillac, a hydraulic river
you fight the ozone**FACES**   the enemy cars   race through the
comikframes   the panels of flat tension   you are a red**SERIES**,
a fury of **COMIK**production   your caption**BODY** rips ideas, plot
you are a stereo**TYPE**   a **NAHUA**grafik   your hair spreads in
shrieking hydraulix   aztlán**EXITS** imageflights   fast **8-BALLS**
roll from your eyes   your xeroxshadows spark in city blocks
markets highways   your teeth are black dice   everyone holds
your body in their hands you laugh in their faces,
shock**SCREAM**

WAKE UP WAKE UP WAKE UP we are workers, this is our
mouthsmoke, our wind, we will **MASS**, will **FLASH**produce our
knowledge, our corn, a furious%, a fuel**RIVER**, a blue**SERIES**
of life+++++++++++++%%%

SERIES SERIES SERIES 99. $3.00 of **WORKER LABOR**
A MANUAL OF ESCAPE AND SECRET   WORKERirony
A TWISTING PLANE OF FORCE DIRECTION RESISTANCE:
++++++++++++++ **SERIES SERIES SERIES 99**.
Splitting roses
Throats of the graphic river
The dislocated heart of motion
mass printed ghetto voices*************+++
        SERIES 99   COMIK BARRIO XEROX

Old School

The field of barrels points to the SKY   campesinofingers moving
UP and DOWN the blueface   they shoot silences into the air
a black cube of speed   a poster of infinite ink   a revolt of
skyFRAGMENTS   a brown army of repetitions   in the chamber
of the RIFLE battalions of lips   heartbarrels   batos vagos
rustling their cotton sweat   their huaraches of sad flesh   bodies
of corn rustling through the river
                    CHOLA MOTHERS   BROWNSKINS
rifleCRACK this square this theater of your tears   riotMOVE
your bellies against the prints   WHO told you it was your saliva
that must glue together the letters of fine writing?
Who told you that you must shovel your bone and laughter, that
you must pick your lips to bullet them into the last stars of
your sleep?
Whose script do you drink at night out of a 40 oz., whose
glass eyes?
Homeboy, homegirl, write ZAPATA on your retinas in your sleep
germ his face from the stalks of your cornrockets   tattoo his face
on your tongues with the splinters of your voices   turn your faces
into metal and obsidian   your corn germs will spread the blue
material of the clouds   this square this poster are yours   this
chamber is the field of your veins   an anthem of rifleEYES
Kill the viral circles of history   your children are not lost   your
hands your brains not erased   you are workerFACES   tell
everyone   your ABUELITA   your FRIEND   your ENEMY   your
FAMILIA   that we must move with windSPEED   a riot of black
space   a shell of rocketing voices   twisting into the white river of
the POSTER   the poster is the WORLD

218

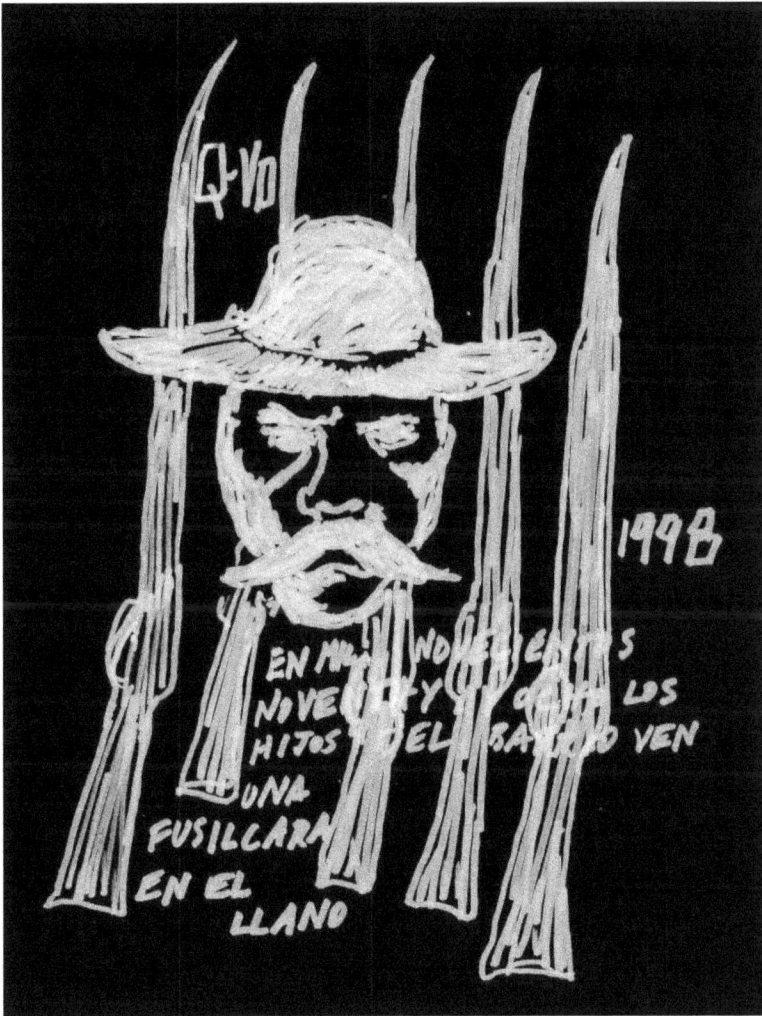

This poster was recovered from the dumpster at Ernie's Label Shop on Broadway Street in Albuquerque, New Mexico. It is rumored that the artist is Fortunio Archuleta, a local man who was responsible for many public art projects in the 1970s, including the Pueblos Memorial in Five Points. Fortunio was committed to the State Psychiatric Ward in 1987 and released a few years later, following massive budget cuts. He now resides in the South Valley of Albuquerque.

Para Mi Hermana en el Día de Pascua
For My Sister, on Easter Day

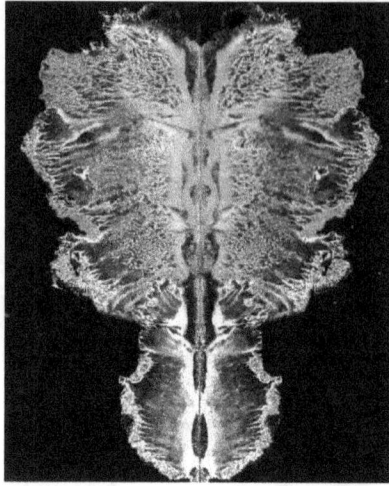

While there is rain in its cup, as new as the
spit from a bay, and while the moon falls in
rivers, all of these things are
emptied from you, pulled on a boat over impermanence,
in the muddy rushes, in
the breaking horizon.

Bird, your throat is full
of light, and it is thin; the voice's tendrils
move in hollow morning, reviving
the hair, glowing in laurel.

This empty mud and plum branch spread
of days is for you
a permanent sun, the familiar, well-walked entrails
of the rose.

Unfold your early linen and your golden earlobes, open
the rosy chambers of your hands, and there find
your stern crucifix, its hard married crosspieces,
it will take from each fingernail a drop
of white blood, firm as mercury
which resists dew
under the sharp beating moon.

With the oil in fields and the rosin of torches
sweet as hay in a panicked bird's stomach
sweet as a forest of crushed greetings
your tender veins go, with
shuffling footsteps, with young linen and experience.

My sister, walk in these roads, feeling your
weight and your silent tongue, remembering
the distances, the repetitions of the moon.
Touch your arms, the branches of a dark star;
touch the density, raveling your plumes, gathering the sky
spread this against
idiot suns, the copper faces that dot mud
across the fins of the sea.

Leave rocks in the sun, fuming its white
ocean with the smell of your hair, its
braids of dried rosemary and *chamiza*.
Go to fields and railroads, my sister, open
your ribs, quiet the foxes, leave space
for the lambs; part the morning in half, and
before everything, next the creatures
of your mother, and father, and sisters and brothers.

For them give your surface of
decreased stars, with a shaking of
tin, the silver water of your fingers.

Between your brother and mockery drive
your wings of joined iron, your spears of water,
your feathers of syllables and
the lyric splinters of your crying.

Go without fear, angel,
with no lies on your
feet, go to the center, in the face of
the empty.
Pierce the palm of shamed
gods, and draw your thread. Leave
meetings of cloud and fevers of
water, leave clover and leave roots of blood.

Sister, the ocean, the sky, the rain, wrap my
body in dusk gold, the burst of your feet, the pure
ridge of your song.

It Writes Itself

Bloodied things relieved against hard stone
      each voice imprinted,
each voice drawn, mouthed,
trailed, bloody in sky—
          deep weltering.

Spoken, a harvest of bruised syllables;
     punctuadas,
cuerdas desgarradas de lamento inquieto;
       ojos violados,
      purple—a headwaters of rain for raked land,
      its pained salinity,
      in furrowed mud.

Each throat unquiet,
       that figure figured in land.
     Prostrate, the earth
       pelo enredado
         canción ensangrentado
I love her,
minister to that beauty,
      darktouched   obscured
Plundered the red earthen limbs
voice earthburied deep interred;

Voice long outpoured
figured out of torn earth graven in
       red
        sky

The Bogeyman Journals { Chapter 22 }

monster monster monster   drumming in the closets of light
in the jungle
jungle jungle jungle   devouring the clouds

monster   where monster   where do I begin   end
white terror   vomiting ash   spitting eyes of light   they have
mutilated my sleep   rat face   dog teeth   a laughing kachina   the
snorting dust   the smoking jaws

a clown of teeth   a whitefaced Indian   with a wounded voice
the meat falls from my body   I am made of long wounds
of flickering hunger   of monster faces vomiting the sun
skinning blood over the rocks   over the smoke   over the treed
depth   toward flame   drunk by the earth
flashTHROWN the coiled rootMIRROR

monster of ugly light   face of beastindian   of bogeyman

jungle jungle jungle bogey bogey   with fingers of plantain
I run without a skin   I catch the little children   I drum with
their eyes   I jaguar over grass   I cut rooster feet   I coil   I death
myself with trees   I run   I run on the pampas   pistols   wind
the gallop of handcuffs   terror   clouds escaping like the sea

the rain running   the eyes crazied

bogey bogey bogeymanned in the closets of ships   handcuffed
in the water   nailed in the rain   and the earth   fierce blackindian
shrieking boar   gorillaed   bogey   nightHACKLED   whipped into
million faces of monster   a smiling pueblo devil dancing with
guitar feet   with leaf hands   abandoned killer   sent to the sea
outside the pueblo   outside the jungle   outside the desert

outside the body   outside light of the planet   outside his dust
face   his face of beastindian   crazied   bogeyed

I am always born with tendons of dreams   of death   clown
my amputated voice   my pupils raining in the stars   terrified
running from myself   through the forest of lightning
through the blood of fireflies   through the swarm of crying
hooves

they want to snuff me out   marines are looking for me   they
have their rifles   yellow hammers of sun   nails   rain   frenzy

masks   masks   masks   they invent me   they invent my devil
nose   my ash eyes   my pig lips

running   white/indio/black   carrying my arrows   fast
my hair in the sky   tied with buffalo tongue   my paws
storming with hunger

they ran me   they chased my eyes   I swallowed my scars
sheltered myself near the candle of death   they mutilated my
journals   I ran over infinite torn cotton of the desert   got rifles
saddles   they took me prisoner

I ran through the favelas of Brazil   the projects of Puerto Rico
the barrios of Mexico

in the temples   in the subways   in the field

I run on motorcycles   through light tunnels   {PUNK METAL}
ripped pig dreams   freakMASKS   last hour escapes   they want
to find me   handcuff   they remember   I remember
it is BOGEYmembered

Los Diarios Cucuy { Capitulo XXII }

monstruo monstruo monstruo tamborileando en los gabinetes
de luz en la selva
selva selva selva devorando las nubes

monstruo DÓNDE monstruo dónde empiezo^acabo terror
blanco vomitando ceniza escupiendo ojos de luz me han
mutilado el descanso cara de rata dientes de perro
una kachina riente el polvo que resopla las mandíbulas
jumeantes

un payaso de dientes un indio de cara blanca con la voz herida
la carne se cae de mi cuerpo estoy hecho de largas heridas
de hambre parpadeante de caras de monstruo vomitando el sol
despellejando la sangre sobre las rocas sobre el humo sobre el
fondo arbolado hacia la llamita bebido por la tierra cucuyada
relampaTIRADA
la raizESPEJO . . . enroscado

monstruo de luz fea cara de indiobestia de cucuy

selva selva selva coco coco con dedos de guineo corro sin
pellejo pesco de nenitos tamborileo con sus ojitos jaguareo la
muerte sobre el pasto corto patas de gallo me enrosco
cambio respiro me muerteo con árboles me pongo el
sombrero corriendo corriendo en las pampas pistolas viento
el galope de las esposas terror nubes fugadas como la mar

comiendo la lluvia los ojos loqueándose

coco   coco   cucuyado en los gabinetes de las naves   esposado
en el agua   clavado en la lluvia en la tierra   morenoindio fierro
javelín chillón   gorileado coco   carne   noche**ERIZADO**   azotada
en mil caras de monstruo   un santo llorón sin ojos   lágrimas
pintadas   un diablo risueño del pueblo bailando con guitarras de
pies   con hojas de manos   un asesino abandonado   mandado al
mar   fuera del pueblo   fuera de la selva   fuera del desierto
fuera del cuerpo   fuera de la luz del planeta   fuera de su cara de
polvo   su cara de indiobestia   loqueado   cucuyado
nazco siempre

con los tendones de sueños   de muerte   payaso   mi voz
amputada   mis pupilas lloviendo en las estrellas   atemorizado
huyéndome de mí   por el bosque de relámpagos   por la sangre
de luciérnagas   por el enjambre de pezuñas lloronas

pintura borroso corriendo   borrascando las voces   los gabinetes
las frutas

me quieren desaparecer   me está buscando la marina   traen sus
rifles   martillos amarillos de sol   clavos   lluvia   frenesí
máscaras   máscaras   máscaras
me inventan   inventan mi nariz de diablo   mis ojos de ceniza
mis labios de puerco

corriendo   blanco/indio/negro   cargando mis flechas   recio
mi pelo en el cielo   atado con lengua de búfalo   mis patas
borrascando con hambre

me corrieron   me persiguieron los ojos   me tragaba las cicatrices
me amparaba cerca de la velita de la muerte   me mutilaban las

memorias   corría sobre el algodón infinito roto del desierto
cogía fusiles   sillas de montar   me tomaron preso
corría por las favelas de Brazil   los caseríos de Puerto Rico
los barrios de México

EL CUCUY VIVE AQUÍ

en los templos   en los subways   en el campo

Corría en motocicletas   por túneles de luz   {METAL PONK}
sueños desgarrados de puerco
máscarasFREAK   escapades de última hora   me quieren hallar
para esposar mis páginas
se acuerdan   me acuerdo   se ACUCUYcuerda   luceshora
SOLESfilosos   hierro borroso

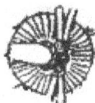

El Torito Rasquache:
Border Restaurant and Inn

Menu:

Roasted Beef
Tequila
Yanqui Stew

Ballads and Pistols
Fortepianos of sky
Breath in a holster
Ash and stirrups
Stingy plates
Picadillo
Sobbing lemons

Alert, cowboy, dangerous times. Hold your reins, the sheriff's
men are coming, saloon of chains. They're already here. Spitting
bandit rumors of Juán Vigil or de la Vara or Ramos Cruz, one
Orozco Peña, one Ignacio Juárez Soledad or Tlacaelel who has
beehive eyes and raucous hands of crossed blood.

Train tracks   asterisks for faces   Guadalupe graffiti

Subcomandante Marcos   cholo time
Yellow cactus   flowers on the mare's neck
bony cowboys flapping their stars and gambler music bootfaced
vigils of bread and sun
rangers explode in mirrors

230

Small candle in the refuge of bees
Small tequila of rooster crowns
Small flutter of Nahua lips:
Reach the bandit, reach the menus of our tears

This saloon's coyote sons will escape the white ash of the wake,
the corrido song, the torch, they become seeds in the water of
mariachi altars, in restaurants of pomegranate and breathing
curtains, in refrains of bearded corn, in the tiny hands that
cotton themselves in extinct lights
of the train

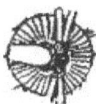

Martinez Lee

martinez lee always wakes up at four o'clock in the morning
she always rubs her eyes and shakes the clouds from her hair
she dresses and puts on special tennis shoes that suit her mood
like a cat she is lonely but she has an understanding of the world
when she walks, the world stretches and offers suggestions:

she sees plum candy, posters of light, a tiny garden of stains on the street,
the faces of animals on windowsills, a private message among the trees,
a cardboard box filled with wind.
rainbow fingers connect her to all points in the world
she starts walking
there are pieces of the moon in her eyes

the morning is cold and dark but it begins to sway like a tide
nobody sees her and she prefers it—this way no one can hear
what she's thinking
no one can see her face and read the river of light that passes
across it each second
the stars gather for a moment to blink a song
everyone begins to wake up
when she gets on the bus, she smiles as she puts a quarter into
the tinkling machine.
the busdriver's question trails in the air: "and how you doing
today young lady?"

later when she gets off the bus, her girlfriends see her and swarm to grab her arms. they are shrieking and their voices and eyes are like popping lights.

she smiles and replies to everything in a whisper.

she walks with them arm in arm.

they form a trolley and disrupt traffic.

all the leaves on the trees are laughing.

martinez has a new life.

suddenly she changes her mind and struggles free,

quietly resisting the lanes of this destiny and its promises.

her skin can sense change around her the way a cat's whiskers feel things in the darkness.

what are the mysteries that life will unwrap?

a man on the street follows her, yelling.

finally he blocks her way, reaches toward her hollering "you're not even that beautiful."

"i can kill you," she says firmly.

startled, he steps away in shadows.

she goes into the library.

memories are pressed together in deep sleep.

martinez can hear their breathing—she opens one of them.

quickly she follows the thoughts that branch from the pages.

they begin to climb and pull—a motion amplified

into the smooth shadows of a snailshell.

the book closes on itself. she hikes to the top of a tall hill in her city and drinks a bottle of juice.

down through the roof of the fog the city is a blue depth filled with reflections.

it moves through her bottle. she coughs and waits.

everything below and around her is so large and so far away.

there is nothing else. she is her only witness.

she would like to swim on this eternity and do nothing but blink.

but what if she could no longer feel things around her?

no, things are better here.

martinez pulls some colored pencils and paper from her bag.

she makes a picture. a swan on hills of snow. a cat climbing a
fire escape ladder.

a girl with red cheeks in a gold field. on the bottom she writes:
a map of my heart.

she writes it in characters, in spanish and in english.

she lets the arms of the wind carry it away like a seed.

she imagines how it will crumble away and flutter down.

the pieces will rain into the laps of old people, they will dissolve
in coffee and gust through teenagers' hair.

the pieces will speak quietly. they will say the things
she can't say.

an unseen hand will collect the whispers and repeat them in the
moonlight on her eyes.

martinez lee, martinez lee, who are you?

what are you hiding from? where are you going?

she wakes up and follows her map in the early mornings.

you may see her:

you will never hold her.

BaRRrio + S = MusicSurplus

NorteñoFACE norteñoFACE   documents documents documents

NorteñoFACE norteñoFACE   documentsdocdocdomentdents

NorteñoFACEnorteñoFACEnor   documents docutracks of eyepaint

NorteñoFACEnort   prints of tongue documents docum

NorteñoFACEnorteñoFACE   scars scars scars water water wind

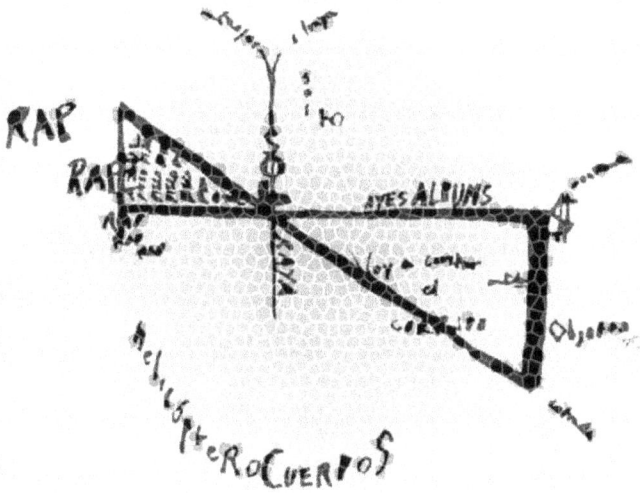

WHO are norteño workers?→
In the varrios in the city in the
palace of light   in the
tournaments of SIGNS in
shops of radiation
throbbing numbers
trailers of sleeping dirt.
The norteño worker is a river of
products, of coins a cash of
movements, a value of twisting
days, a solid cube of future

angels, a ray of maquiladora

birth, a streak of buzzing eyes

an exported wound, a meteor of throats

a boxed struggle

twilightMATERIAL+objectFACE+

He makes→

NIKE + clothing + rain of fingers→ his hands are trains exporting
fruits of sweat

tropicWHISPERS nerves of water→ tubers, agave, bananas, sugar,
NIKEsleep

WHO are norteñoCHILDREN?→

RAP rap RAP wires of silver shout from speakers gulfs of
albumFLIGHT fingers of megaHERTZ flashingBANDS rippling
over skies buildings markets new stereoIRIS falling into windows,
speakerFISTS driving into words of cotton, through linen memories
RADIOwounds invisible TEARS signals moving in STEREOcrops
redSAMPLEbirds

Young norteño children→ form + shake + shoot out a surplus of
fused strings + bulbs + blending lyric iron→

Motors of wireLOVE tracks of humming fruit STREAMS of impulse
HOW do norteño children move through the offices of the sky, the
crystals of the market?→ they helicopterOPEN money they spread
the violins of their lips a cross spins in the ear a flower of shadow
SPLITS the throat they sing SING rap they crack the
OBJECTboxes they crack their productFACES they barbACT
surplus surplus desire that overWIRES the sky

Canción

My voiceflower
Here are your five songs
My birdflower
Tree humming through the night
Eyes rimmed with lashes
Giving birth to the rain's dark hands
Here is your body beside me
Your sweat like moonlight's snails
My bleeding-rainbow flower
My whitestoneflower
Your lover travels through your dream to find you
Singing
Child of flowers
Sweet one that you are, my own:
Here
This is where I am
I am here

Mi flor de voces
Tienes cinco canciones
Mi flor de pájaros
Tu arbol zumbando la noche
Mi flor de pestañas
Dando nacer a las manos oscuras de la lluvia
Mi flor de cuerpo desnudo
Tu sudor los caracoles de la luz de luna
Mi flor de arcoírises que sangran
Mi flor de piedras blancas
Tu amante camina a través de tu sueño, buscándote
Te está cantando, mi niña de flores
Mi niña   mi niña de flores
Estoy aquí   estoy aquí   estoy aquí

The Counterfeiters

they did not stalk they only watched
they floated like leaves on the surface of life
their laughter was like bones of the tongue chiming   they
befriended shadows
the colors of blood   sorrow   oranges in the night   parakeets
at the closing of day their profiles slanted into
the foreheads of stone
on each one's belly the day rippled in a different form

they could only speak in emotions   each kind was different
a symphony of radiant glyphs
they did not share or hide this movement
but let it be what it might be in the tide of surfaces

they preferred happiness but they knew pain
they found the wombs of feeling at the far places
or deep below layers of the world   they found that some were
too powerful
some of their kind became different
they lost their skin and dragged their exposed nerves behind them
in flaming whips
they released hurricanes of scars against the faces of the sky
and earth
they confronted humans with the blackened roots of
their voices
with totems of blood   with changing masks that sang fear and
praise

they could not think
but through feeling again and again the shapes of life
the rules of its eternal outward folding   they learned
they found how things were ordered and eroded
they touched the skull of a horse   the green star of a cactus
the pulsing bloom of an embryo   the ghosts that raced
across nets of silicone
some stayed   some fled across the snailshells of space
some simply floated and felt as the world guided
its warm passion   its snarling violence
some found that no octave of emotion could survive across the
rifts of cloud and sea
they struggled as they must
they grew arms that could encircle the wild machetes of
the rainbows
the ripping of mirrors   the sparks of the water avalanches
some were trapped in expressions of porcelain and acrylic
some remained hidden in the sleep of life as spirits of ignition
exploding   in angels of force   they lit the sky
they gleamed in the boards of life
humans whispered and could not explain certain things
who knows how it happened?   i was lucky   it was a miracle
some chose happiness above all things
they raised it in unending pylons   it remains among us
we gather to it as to a bonfire
we wonder when it can be sung awake or we possess it like lovers
in the drift of dark lights something tenses
it shimmers fierce points   we breathe differently
it surrounds us

Within

i wonder how other people make love
what it is like for them
is it like running toward the sun
into the storm of burning snow?
is it like the throbbing of a hundred cuts on the fingers
placed under a waterfall of tears?
is it like the hunger of a bear
who has slept beneath groaning roots all winter
while her children gnaw at her breasts?

days when I was a boy running among weeds taller than me
i heard the boys on the corner talk about girls

when i was seven
i went to Mexico City to do Aztec dances
we worshipped the Sun and the Feathered Serpent
all day long barefoot on the hot street
my *maestro* told me in the Nahua dances
you must sacrifice
that night i dreamt that i was completely inside the body
of one of the *maestras*
there was a light
i could see her spine
and her ribs
i felt a stab of pleasure that shook me awake for a moment
and then i slept again

is it like a wound crying?
when you bristle   and bronze circles fall from the night

do the petals of your face fall away?
when taste changes from milk to cinnamon
from water dunes to salt
the doors of the ocean open
beneath me   within you

when I visit my friend from Cuba, New Mexico
the words don't matter
we watch the people move
we watch Buffalo Brother
we watch

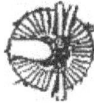

If You Leave

You hang up the phone. You think of his hands, roses uprooted from the dark earth. You think of him lying on the couch, his face a star in flames, his smile of hope. You go to the corner of your room. There, with a window on each side, like tall wings of glass, is an altar where you have put letters, photos, tiny bottles of silver, milagros—animals of mud with fierce eyes. You light a blue veladora and the sticker of the Virgen María moves with shadows beneath the flame. You put your hands together with fingers crossed and sit. You wait for hours. The windows throw white cubes of afternoon into your room, then red faces of twilight, purple sheets that hang from the ceiling. You get up and go to the phone again. You beep the ten buttons and your lover answers. You talk for a moment about nothing, then you tell her. That the end of your father happened fast.

Oh, my God, are you okay? she cries.

You ask her quietly if she will be there for you.

Let's talk about something else, about your father.

Of the things you hope from her, there are some she said you cannot ask. Months ago, she wanted you to move away with her. You told her you could not because you had to take care of him, his glowing body that lay on the couch, his laughing smile: he was your son now, your father was your child.

You can't do this to me, she had said, *if you leave me I'll kill myself   I have the bottle of pills in my hand right now*

242

Comets that passed through your head, beside your father's as he calmly told you *Go mi'jo, go away for school, go live with her. I am getting better.* You said no, but his gentle strength won with silence. *Go, mi'jo, I want you to.*

You hold the phone to your ear. Things you cannot ask. You say all right and speak for a while and she wishes you well and you hang up. You return to the altar. Papi's eyes fill the room with dark light. The stars and the night join you. Your room is alive with rays and shadows, a dance from the gathering mountains, the twisting trees, the animals of dirt and snow, the clouds, the water trickling. You light another candle.

On the altar, you bring together the photo of her and the photo of him. You do not smell ashes, you smell only his rose hands, burning.

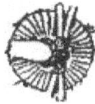

Jaguar House

Joselito is awake at 6 a.m. in sweat   he drags his body into his
clothes   he takes his rent money from the drawer   he walks in
darkness down 16th Street to Shotwell   the windows of his car
are broken   he dusts glass onto the street and sits   he revs the
engine and begins to drive   he has not slept in four nights   he
stops for coffee   his car is a humming bomb   it snarls as he
pours gasoline into its throat   it shatters the yellow dashes
*Querida Mami, no me aguanto, me urge ir a casa de Papi/Dear
Mami, I can't take it, I have to go to Papi's house*
Bakersfield and Needles and Jackrabbit   I-40   the Mojave's
jaws are the brown and yellow *temazcal* that cooks his brain
his dreams sweat   they clutch the linen in the motel bed   he
awakens and there is blood in his ears   wasps of glass pierce
his nose   tongue
the sleep pounds his eyes   two days
He begins again at 2:30 a.m.   he has passed the weigh station
when he sees a fire   the night writhes in flames   the darkness
burns forty feet high   its flesh turns into the cloud of stars
Smells of death follow Joselito   the burning hands flap
the car smiles and invites them
Joselito guns the motor until it screams
Joselito reaches New Mexico
He goes to Cochiti   he pulls a carp from the lake and cuts its
jade lips   he cuts the tongue from a cow   the red malachite
and the green fins   he wears them like a song on his neck
In Albuquerque he burns cash for a pistol   he gets the old
heavy one
The car howls
He crosses the Rio Bravo   brown faces in the slabs of water

244

He reaches his father's address
The branches of darkness over the house   stillness breathing
like a quiet figure in the yard
woven water dripping   the smell of rain on leaves   wet *piñon*
the shadows drunk with crickets   the weeds strange as flowers
Joselito reaches the door and searches for the key under stone
Nothing
roots   and wooden shells
He caresses the door handle and tries to force it
Nothing
He presses his cheek to the door   he can smell his father's
memory through the crack   he can hear the laughter
glimmering the fireplace   he can see the walls blue purple and
red as his father painted them
Déjame pasar, Papi.   Llévame contigo, por favor.
Let me in, Papi.   Take me with you, please.
The wind groans cottonwoods   the moon's hands slither
Joselito repeats and repeats
He caresses the gun
He cries gasoline knives onto the porch   he leans his head on
the hands of adobe
He stands before the jaguar house   the gold flares of the ears
the blue tombs of the nostrils
the wooden doors of the claws
He asks to be taken with his father
He cannot enter
At the pawnshop the old gun changes into two wrinkled bills.
Joselito drinks coffee.
The car's teeth melt into fiends of laughter

Phoenix Hotel

Joselito dogs the highway from Vegas to Los to San Pancho
the car grinds its metal heart
its eyes bleed crystal   *Don't hurt yourself*
At the Golden Gate Bridge the sky falls in oceans
silks white red   a dying chrysanthemum
¿Y ahora dónde?/Now where?
The car leads   detouring the night strips   the torches of the
Embarcadero   Stockton's dragon throat   Batongbacal St
Purificación St   Centeotl St   to Shotwell
Stop and park   the car shivering like an addict
Joselito doesn't feel home
He goes to the gas station for coffee
He remembers something
He runs home through the side to avoid the rent hounds
In his room he searches his coats
A paper leaflet   *Gathering of the Arts: 6th Sun*
He returns to the car but it is roasting black   the hood blistered
Estás loco/You're crazy
He walks down Mission to the place   some hotel in
Filipino Town
At the door Cookie Losa from San José wearing a Kangol crusher
Hey, loquito she hugs him
Joselito has forgotten how to speak   he looks at her with empty
eyes   she gives him a discount   he goes inside   down the hallway
sprayed with graffiti   photos of San Cristobal and Manila   into
the dark auditorium
On the stage Eun Joo Cheung   darkness braided around her face
her head lifts upward   she sings Arirang slowly
a thousand years pouring   a moon on the sand   streams of wood

Joselito cries gold leaves

The lights go on. The furious applause rains on the faces.

Someone else on the stage. The mic crackling nervous   *We will be having intermission*

In the half-light Joselito begins to see faces he knows

he chokes pale *I am a ghost I don't belong*

But the faces come   the hands they talk

Fofo "Serve the People" Cazares with his tree trunk arms   *This is my boy right here*

Nura Lim the political grandmother of Chinatown   *So nice to see you!*

Naheed the shaggy thinker   *I must follow you around next time*

Milton Wai the indie cowboy   *Sei ba po! Sei ba po!*

Becky "What the Deal" Chi   *I'm having a barbecue please come this Sunday*

Damon Sagrado   *Man where the hell you been you missed my cd release party, fool*

Toni "Crazy Girl" Miyoshi (on a bullhorn)   *Three Dollar shots at the bar! Three Dollar shots at the bar! THREE DOLLAR SHOTS AT THE BAR!!!*

Blinding laughs   radiant lips   he is a king. *I am back from the dead*   he claps stunning flashes

Jenni Nam smacks him in the chest and hands him a drink

Joselito clangs his glass against Milton's *Lei ho!*   he begins running   cameras snapping

Cigarettes outside   fountains of gold liquor   ancient darkness quiet songs

Let's go back inside

Joselito sees Melanie   his best friend from San José   they love one another like sisters   before she can say hi he runs to the bathroom and with the two pangs of his hands takes his last written paper from his pocket and folds it   folds it again in the

shape of a temple   and comes out and gives it to her   she takes a
moment from spinning records

I'm so glad to see you Lito   she looks at the paper and says *I
dreamt this moment before did you know I love temples and in
the dream there was a big cat i'm just so glad to see you and it's a
trip cuz I know I've known you before and that Tres Flores stuff
you use in your hair reminds me of my grandmother man I
missed you*

Then she's back to spinning and she takes a moment to come out
to bounce crazy dub rasta to kiss with her girlfriend to tip her
cap to Joselito

Music surrounding body flames

Jenni Nam is back with new mobs of friends   Joselito's smile
passes through solitudes and beating hair to reach them

Nice to meet you

Jenni points to the stage   *We should dance up there   bring
some water too*

Legs coiling   heaving phoenix rays
at first only a few are moving   like children
then everyone is dancing

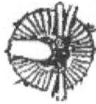

Noches de Conjunto

Esta tarde que hubo un viento seco y la noche se iba bajando por
el desierto, vinieron otra vez. Fue un milagro terrible, así como el
nacimiento de Tonatiuh, como las rosas que corrieron por las
manos de San Juan mientras él miraba hacia Su cara relumbrante,
como el águila que desgarró una culebra sobre un nopal mientras
los mexica esperaban. Eran las cuatro o las cinco, la polvareda
estuvo llena de sombras y fuego, y la carretera se estremecía como
un cascabel negro. Nadie se acuerda dónde pasó; puede que fue
Sinaloa, o Chihuahua; algunos dicen que fue en Laredo, otros en
Mixoacan. Hasta hay gente que dice que lo vio en la central de
Los Angeles. Occurrió así: por allá en la linea del cielo se veía
acercarse un tren que escupía y chillaba, bajándose como el fin
del mundo. Venía lentamente, más lento, hasta que se paró,
bufando y pitando, sacudiéndose con cadenas y royendo los
carriles. Aunque no hubo ninguna estación, cuatro figuras se
bajaron del tren y empezaron a caminar por la arena: estaban
vestidos al estilo charro, con sombreros, botas, espuelas y
zahones, y camisas oscuras: cargaban bolsas de cuero y cosas
cubiertas de serapes: sus caras estaban ocultadas bajo sus paños, y
sus ojos relumbraban.

Los cuatro caballeros se pararon en una loma arenosa y
empezaron a desatar sus bolsas y bultos, agachados, arreglando
sus cosas en montones oscuros. Uno de ellos miró a los otros y
dio tres cabezadas. Fue entonces que sucedió: lo impensable, el
milagro terrible. Echaron sus sombreros y gritaron, sus ojos
echando fuego y espuelas de luz, sus voces claras y violentas,
como diamantes que se rajaban. Uno de ellos apretó su acordeón
y de ello salió una nube temblante de chispas y voces blandas:

Otro levantó sus brazos y empezó a aporrear su batería. El tercero desgarró su guitarra y de sus manos manaron lamentos eléctricos. El cuarto empezó a cantar las palabras del viejo corrido que hizo que la noche y el día se mezclaran y derramaran brasas por la cara del desierto.

Se quedaron cante y cante. Su canción fue el primer recuerdo del cielo, su tristeza más larga, su maldición más relampagueante y ahumada. Mientras tocaban, sus cuerpos y voces formaron cuatro puntos: una estrella, una brújula, un reloj de sol. Relucieron en una cruz, girando como una llave que le quemaría las tuercas a la ultima llanta de caucho de todo el mundo y la mandaría a los tingos.

Era conjunto puro. Dentro de su columpio y su golpizo habían serpientes de rock 'n roll desde Teotihuacán, azotando fugas y terror fronterizo: mecate y herraduras: ferrocarriles que se reían, vidrio roto: el humo y las luces de un bar desbaratado: el zumbido de un cadilac narcotraficante: olor a pino y nopal, platos calientes de taquillos y rebanaditas: el *chinga tu madre* del último pachuco: la garganta derretida de la última balada: un retrato de un Elvis prieto: las arpas centellantes del son jarocho, las flores de nopal destellándose en el lloriqueo de trompetas Garibaldi: los sollozantes pulmones aterciopelados de una princesa *blues:* superficies ásperas de Stetson: trasfondos azules de mate: una gota de sangre sobre una bota de pellejo'e culebra.

Luego gente de todas partes empezó a acudir: llegaron abuelitas enredadas en sus rebozos que dejaron obsequios en frente de los caballeros del conjunto. Dejaron velas, misterios, amor: dejaron sus corazones y sus rosarios; dejaron fotos de sus maridos e hijos desaparecidos. Viejos pachucos y tecatos llegaron y dejaron

paños de algodón con retratos de Jesucristo hechos a tinta:
lloraron y pidieron perdón: dejaron sus agujas y sus pistolas.
Vinieron braceros que se quitaron sus sombreros: que enjugaron
sus lágrimas con sus manos hinchadas y cicatrizadas, y dejaron
bolsas de chile piscado. Alguien parqueó su *lowrider* delante de
los caballeros y se lo dejó. Una pareja jóven empezó a bailar
quebradita, torciendo y sacudiéndose, hasta que el chamaco se
lastimó la espalda, y se pararon aún sonriendo. Todo mundo
empezó a murmurar: *los dioses del sol, los dioses del sol, los
dioses del sol.*

Luego el cantante principal se quitó el paño de la cara, sus
dientes gatunos reluciendo como vidrio, sus ojos *bebop* blancos y
furiosos, su chaleco de cuero temblando, y dijo algo en el viejo
idioma del llano y el nopal y el cascabel que nadie pudo
comprender: echó plumas por las cabezas de la gente, de sus
narices corría incienso blanco. Luego dio un botazo, se puso su
sombrero, y el conjunto se subió otra vez el tren, sus caras de
retablo aún tocadas por la luz rosada de las velas, sus
instrumentos echando lamentitos de hierro. El tren empezó a
bombear y silbar, y la noche llenaba los ojos de toda la gente, y
todos supieron que la venganza del desierto se había acabado.
Los cuatro duendes habían pasado por este mundo.

Veía todo esto mientras me sentaba con mi amigo Ysidro y
tomábamos cervezas. Lo he visto más de una vez, y vendrán más
noches de conjunto. Así es como viene el milagro terrible—la
tarde se está acabando: hay un viento seco, y la noche se baja por
el desierto.

Conjunto Evenings

In the dry wind as night fell on the desert, they came again. It was maybe four or five, the dust was filled with shadows, the highway quivered like a black rattle. It might have been Sinaloa, or Chihuaha: some say it was in Laredo, others San Diego. A train came from the distance, spitting and screaming, coming down like the end of the world. It began to slow, whinnying and stamping, shaking chains and chewing the tracks. Though there was no station, four figures climbed out of the train and began walking out into the sand. They wore *sombreros*, boots, spurs, chaps, and dark shirts: they carried leather bags and *serapes*, their faces hidden under *paliacates*. Their eyes were gleaming.

The four horsemen stopped on a hill and hunched over their dark bundles, pulling things out. One of them nodded three times. Then they threw off their hats and screamed, their eyes streaming fire and spurs of light, their voices cracking like diamonds. One of them squeezed trembling clouds from his accordion: Another struck his drums again and again. The third slashed his guitar and from his hands came electric wails. The fourth began to sing the words of the old *corrido* that made the night and day mix and spill embers over the face of the desert.

They sang and sang. Their song was the sky's earliest memory, its longest sadness, its smokiest flashing curse. As they played, their bodies and voices formed four points: a star, a compass, a sun clock. They glimmered in a cross, spinning like a lug wrench that would burn the screws off the last rubber wheel and send them to the devil.

It was pure *conjunto*. Inside its swinging and its thumping there were rock 'n roll serpents from Teotihuacan, whipping flights of border terror: rope and horseshoes: laughing train tracks, broken glass: the smoke and lights of a rundown bar: the humming of a drugdealer cadillac: the smell of pine and cactus, hot plates of *taquillos* and *rebanaditas*: the *chinga tu madre* of the last pachuco: the melting throat of the last ballad: a portrait of a Brown Elvis: the shimmering harps of *son jarocho*, cactus flowers exploding in the whine of Garibaldi trumpets: the sobbing velvet windpipes of a blues princess: rough Stetson hats: blue matte backgrounds: a drop of blood on a snakeskin boot.

Then from nowhere people began to come: grandmothers covered with their shawls began to arrive and leave offerings at the feet of the *conjunto* horsemen. They left candles, mysteries, love: they left their hearts and rosaries: they left photos of their lost husbands and children. Old *pachucos* and *tecatos* came and left cotton *paños* with ink drawings of Jesus Christ: they cried and asked forgiveness: they left their needles and guns. *Braceros* came and took off their hats: they wiped away tears with their swollen, scarred hands, and left bags of picked *chile*. Someone parked his lowrider in front of the horsemen and left it there. A young couple began to dance *quebradita*, twisting and thrashing, until the boy hurt his back and then they stopped, still smiling. Everyone began to chant: *los dioses del sol*, the sun gods: *los dioses del sol, los dioses del sol*.

Then the lead singer pulled down his *paliacates*, his cat teeth gleaming like glass, his bebop eyes furious and white, his cowhide vest shaking, and he spoke something in the old language of the plains and the cactus and the rattle that no one could understand: he threw feathers over everyone's head and from his nostrils came white incense. Then he stamped his boot, put on his *sombrero*, and the *conjunto* boarded the train again, their altar faces still touched by red candlelight, their instruments letting out iron cries. The train began to pump and hiss, and the night began to fill everyone's eyes, but the desert was motionless. Everyone knew that the four *duendes* had passed through this world.

I watched all of this as I sat with my friend Ysidro and we drank beers. I have seen it many times, and there will be many more *conjunto* evenings. This is how it begins—the afternoon is ending: there is a dry wind, and the night comes down over the desert.

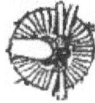

Speaksalone

My name is Speaksalone. I'm from the Havasupai in the Grand Canyon. Sometimes I dance the ram dance with my people. One time I put on the white paint and put on the horns and when I danced there was lightning in the ground. But the next time I put on a dress and I was one of the girls that move by the side of the rams. My long hair carried the night inside of it. I sang softly and I was a girl.

I'm Speaksalone. You can tell I'm different. I'm not a guy or a girl. I have no sex, no organs. I was born that way. Some of the elders say it's because there's pollution in the Grand Canyon, you know? Because our people are being contaminated. Some say it's because I have a special job to do.

When I was little I would speak to myself and I would say things that no one could understand, like in another language. But one of my uncles, he got mad at me. He used to drink a lot. He made me take off my clothes. He told me I was bad, that I was a devil. He made me touch him. I looked at him and I didn't say anything. But then he got scared and ran away. He never did that again.

I always wondered who I was and what I was here to do. To help my people? To change into something else, like an insect? When people would understand that I had no sex, they would open their mouths and poison would come out. Sometimes men wanted to rape me, to break an opening in me. Sometimes they only wanted to laugh at me. Sometimes they were afraid I was a witch spirit. The women were afraid of me too. Some of them wanted me to be like them. Or just to be a man.

I am not a toxic poison. I am not a witch spirit or a sky spirit. I am Speaksalone.

I am walking close to you.

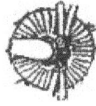

El Duende

there's no money
no food
no hay comida
no hay dinero
run
you better run
run
you better run
catch you some food
you better better
you better
steal if you have to
run down the block
the moon spits some angry slang on the sidewalks
hop the metal fence
run through some angry broken windows
hey, rob the next one you see
the next sister brother
get 'em
get it
take it
helicopters cutting the sky
you start coughing up bad dreams
do it now
don't wait
right there
that dude right there in the basketball court
kneeling down
get that dude
take what he has
or you won't eat

cuz there's nothing left
so you go up
you make your hand into a gun and point it at his head

give it to me
give
me money, food
the dude in the basketball court
he's on his knees
he's looking at you with wide eyes
he's sweating
he's smiling
he's crazy
he's pointing at the sidewalk
he starts laughing and screaming
he throws his hands up

you look at the concrete where he is sitting
he drew something there
a heart   that turns into a flower that turns to a bird
You feel your chest spinning, your mouth is filled with
cold sweat
you hear the helicopters above
you go blind underneath the white fires
they shine on you
damn you better steal you better you better
fast now you
look down but the dude ain't there
he's gone the red heart is gone from the sidewalk
you don't know where it went

now you see, now you see
the dude wasn't crazy
he just refused to take from anybody

he just opened himself to something
you want it to happen to you too
so you take a piece of glass and cut your hands open
it hurts but you stream lyrics of blood all over the concrete
you draw a heart

Turning Into a Butterfly

braid your black hair
wear earrings
don't get a tattoo
exchange clothing for food
roll your old old mexican blanket
keep the wool smell near you
cross the bridges
admire the darkness
fall in zigzags across the sky
find the lights   *maborosi*
kneel   search until your arms shake from thirst
give thanks
everything has a water to drink
run through the caves of darkness between the pine trees
come to the sidewalks
hover near the voices
move between the thoughts
follow   taste the images
gather layers until you have made wings
break the honeycomb of dawn
suck the pieces
search the rain of faces
the music that burns your tongue
crash on the foam   night float
drink from the roots of anger   pity   embraces   sorrow
when you are tired
sleep with the frost lights
the cold fire of grapefruits

awaken
tremble and laugh with the gold rooster in the sky
grow fins
thank souls   old   young
for a gift:
leave your laughter

Coyauqui Journey

On her fifth day of wandering, Coyauqui was blinded by the desert. She fell from cliffs of sand and the night wrapped her so that she could not move her spirit. But finally she saw the river of the sky dancing on her eyelids. Its white antlers held the black moon and threw lightning over everything. Coyauqui stopped wandering. She saw a forest of white corn and she entered. *Coyote, please give me laughter,* she said. *Toad, please give me earth to live and green mud to eat. Snake, swallow me and turn me inside out so that I can be one with the leaves. Crane, open the floors of the sky so I may travel farther. Goldfish, weave a blanket of reflections for me so that I can change as you change.* All of her sisters gave her their gifts, but they did not heal the drowned flowers of her heart.

Coyauqui could go no farther. She spoke to her mother. *Mother, why am I alone.*

I left my place to care for father.

Father has died, his voice does not burn in the pyramids of rain.

My lover has died, she could not breathe without my fingers on her face.

My place is gone, it has gone away with the dizzy winds.

When I came to our house, the deer were screaming. They ate fire and cracked their hooves against the wind. The yellow hurricane of their teeth tore the world. They cried blood and the roots of their antlers burned and ran into the caves. There is nothing left, Mother.

How can I live?

Mother spoke, she called to Coyauqui from below and above.
**Coyauqui, the fields are your spirit. The dust that shines
through your doors. The sun that drums your throat. You did
not lose your loved ones. They were never there to lose. Things
have changed, but it is only that the hand of the earth has
moved. We are change, Coyauqui.**

But how will I change?

**You will find your heart, daughter. You have forgotten your
heart. You will remember something that you have forgotten.**

Coyauqui sat in the world. She tried to remember. *Please I will
remember let me I must I want I will not want I forget*

She waited she saw the iris pumping light under the water
that is my heart
On the blue stalk of the sky, she saw the rays of the crane
that is my heart
Ahead of her she saw the earth turn its mouth up and the savila
plant moved
In the savila plant, that is my heart

My heart, said Coyauqui   she drank the savila   she drank the
spiny leaves   the green mirrors
Now I will swim   now I will fly

Coyauqui returned to her journey

Elegy for Ronnie Burk

Red lions are crawling from the sun's throat
    For Ronnie
The Lady of Dolphins drops needles from the typhoons
    of her eyes
    For Ronnie
The butterflies of Tehuantepec razor toward beaches of ice
    in the North
    For Ronnie
Meteors of roses fall across the Golden Gate Bridge
    For Ronnie

Ronnie has died   Ronnie is gone
Ronnie Jaguar Queen of sand with a dress of pearl rivers
with eyes of burning diamonds
Ronnie
Ronnie an insect of blue jade quivering on the mind's window
Ronnie
Ronnie as strong as the bronze stars sung by Indio
fathermother
Ronnie

The ghosts of the horses run in a halo for Ronnie
the Mexican fiddles curl the leaves of the wind
and the parrot's feathers
a gold and turquoise pot holds Ronnie's whispers

Ronnie who held me when I was a baby
Ronnie
Ronnie who was a Lady

Ronnie
Ronnie who fought the shadows of his heart
Ronnie

Tonight the pages of
the sky's music
fall quietly
To our hands

Heart of Rice Paper

inside is a dragonfly
    a field of candles
    the red rain of beans
    the teeth of blue corn
inside are the panting drums of the bulls
    the lanterns of newborn fingers
    a gold moon tumbling on purple silk
    the cracked flood of the mountains
    a harp of deer throats
inside is a bird with no face that opens wings and stops sound
    a cricket that touches its burning shadow
    the secret of lips pressing and hands whispering
    a guitar that bleeds a yellow lotus
inside are the tiny bones of the sea
    the shriek of the hummingbird that drinks
inside is something and then it is gone
    the sand of crushed snakeskins
    the footprints of the rain
inside is the ink of crows on a white sky
    the mirror of the evening that you polish with a blanket
        of flame
    the mouth of the earth and the ear of the water
    the stairs of silence and the maze of laughter
inside is the circle of pollen where the fury of colors begins
    a buffalo tears through the burning rice and turns white
    an owl floats on the eyes of the water and eats them
    a theater of chanting cranes
inside is a crescent smile and it is a mother
    the hive of children's murmurs

a jaguar that devours the fishscales of the dawn
a tear that breaks lightning on the wind
a green shadow on a tongue
inside something is born and it is gone and it is born again

can you hold your heart between your hands?
can you find it again though you still hold it?
can you fill your heart with the breath of a child?
can you stand before it and be a woman?
can you free its struggling coils into the wild flames of grass
and accept a single grain in your palms?

mahal kita
saranghae
yollopoliuhqui
love is in all things
there is only love

Alcatraz

we rolled out before dawn   nobody said anything
the highway buried lights in our eyes
   when we got to the edge of the earth   we took the ferry
  the sky burned in the water
        the seagulls rose and fell   like crying notes
we came to the island   already there were people
   some were barefoot
we spread out a Pendleton   we put white corn on it   we put
   the *ahumador* in the center
we burned sage and *copal*
       the sun flew up like a thunderbird
we waited until the nations had gathered
   then we pulled out the drums
         puma sister smiling teeth under black eyes
       shadow bird hopping the sky
     buffalo brother cracking white twigs under his hooves
i do not sing   i am better at drums   pound the tree's heart beat
   the hollow wind
        for sticks i use polished bones
  gleaming as the morning darkens
   and the eyes rain memory
      o remember us now
       give us seeds of sweetgrass
     o life before my life   i remember you
      give us our place   among the copper leaves
  the flowers of death   the rainbow of the catfish   that we eat

singing bursts over the island
    shaking the rock's broken spine   its iron hair
the grasses rise from blood and silence   on the prison
     they tremble now   Dine screams   Ojibwe screams
    Ohlone screams
shackles clanging
    Lakota screams
     Blackfoot screams
Yaqui screams
my hair grows down my back
    flowing
dead names   i open my mouth
a coyote strangled in my throat
     escapes   flies
       screaming
    across alcatraz
white arrows stream
from our ears   red corn fills
    our hands

back to the ferry   goodbye for now   back to the land
we drive to the youth gathering   it is night at a house
    in Oakland
     the windows like *luminarias* in the darkness   the cars
      piled over the hills
    boys and girls of the tribes   arriving in caravans
     blood of the four directions   Fijian   Dine
     Purépecha   Zuñi

Pilipino   Shoshone   Korean faces
      hair braided around faces of brown fire   wearing
turquoise on the neck
          rap sounds   reggae sounds
     the drumming continues   faint   in our dances
   hips rolled outwards   in a circle of sparks   shoulders
    turned up slowly
           a great happiness folds us
       with its soft fingers
    we smoke the old spirit   of plants
  the hot cloud spreads   from one mouth to another
        the clusters of laughter   opening their leaves
    tribes speaking quietly   one to another
  islander people   someone shouts   a song
     the voices answer   booming love

List of Illustrations

Acknowledgments

Huge thanks to my cherished friend, artist and author Jarrett Earnest, who brought great insight and sensitivity to our conversations as I developed *Book of Itzolin*. Kurt Wallace Martin also read early sections and gave arrow-perfect suggestions.

Special thanks to all who enriched this book with memories: Itzolin's siblings Karina Marin, Stefan Armstrong, Shifra Pride Raffel, and Kezia; Benjamin Carp; Nikko Harada; Kuusela Hilo; Greg Jackson; Eric Manolito; Kim Mizuhara: Mari Dubedåre Ravndal; John Reamer; Gabriela Spears-Rico; and Truong Tran.

The ranchera Itzolin sang to himself on his audiotapes, page 153, was first called "Voy en Busca de un Mariachi." Later the title was changed to "Plaza Garibaldi." Its songwriter was the late [Enrique] Franco Aguilar, lyricist and composer of many years for Los Tigres Del Norte. Originally, Editora Cronos published the song in Mexico. I owe thanks to three people who especially assisted my quest for permission to quote the lyrics: Rodolfo Gutierrez at San Antonio Music Publishing provided leads. Señor Ángel Hernández at Promosongs International—formerly of Cronos—kindly shared his crucial knowledge of the musicians and history of the copyright. My greatest appreciation goes to Señor Mario Sanchez.

Muchísimas gracias, 440 Music Publishing and Señor Mario Sanchez, for gracious permission to quote the lyrics to "Voy en Busca de un Mariachi," now called "Plaza Garibaldi."

Heartfelt thanks to Robert Sucher for exceptionally generous support of this project, and also to Reyes Cárdenas, James Cha, Denise Chávez, Isabel González, Marie Henry, Chuy Martínez, Catalina Perez, Cynthia Rowberg, Emelle Sonh, Truong Tran and Tim Whiten for their warm encouragement.

Itzolin Presente.

Notes

My Name Means Volcano

p. 28. What Itzolin Does in the Morning: Rises, greets his family and the sun, dresses, puts away his pajamas, eats, combs his hair, brushes his teeth, kisses Mami, Cielo and Oraibi, goes to school.

The Melting of Ymerr's Frost

p. 42. Jack in Irons: According to Yorkshire legend, Jack-in-Irons was a giant to beware of on deserted roads. He even wore the heads of those he attacked! Itzolin had also been fascinated since early childhood by Nordic myths of Ymir, the first being, based on Storri Sturluson's thirteenth-century Icelandic *Prose Edda.*

Journal Excerpts

p. 69. I pray that she appreciates it: I had seen a few excerpts of this remarkable novella, which Itzolin wrote on my old Olympia typewriter. I asked whether he was writing about the same characters at various times. He said, "I don't know, and I don't want the reader to know, either. It's about each moment individually and what someone brought to it." I see intriguing new things in this piece every time I read it.

Face Hanging Like a Star

p. 92. A rapid *samsara:* In Buddhist thought, the endless cycling of birth and rebirth, with all its implied suffering and wandering through successive states.

Itzolin's Answers to Online Questionnaire

p. 138. I received this long questionnaire in the early 2000s and passed it on to family and friends. Itzolin set us all an example by changing the questions to fit his desired answers.

p. 142. Hvil i fred Itzolin, jeg vil alltid huske deg og ditt smil, til vi møtes igjen! /Rest in peace Itzolin, I will never forget you and your smile. Til we meet again! (Norwegian, from cousin Mari)

Itzolin Audiotape Excerpts

p. 147. Apparently Itzolin suddenly left town in October, 2002 and drove all the way to the house in Albuquerque where our family had lived when he was a child. His father still remained there until his death about eight months before this drive. Itzolin had considered doing his Master's thesis on his father's poetry, translating to and from Spanish, but it was a vague idea, wrapped in grief.

Why did Itzolin make these tapes? Did he talk to himself to stay awake? To review his life and befriend it in a hard moment? To leave a record? Maybe all of those things. It's also unknown whether anyone else was ever in the car. When he returned to San Francisco, he told me he hadn't answered his phone because he was sick.

His speech on the tapes is of a young man speaking to a friend. I don't know if he thought I would be the one in charge of the tapes when he left this world, but he must have wanted them found.

The first draft took me over eight months to transcribe, and I went to a therapist to get through it. I used the method I had learned working in research, transcribing every single sound, such as *er, um, like, man,* and occasional stuttering. Later I did a second pass, deleting half of those, also from the training method.

For this book I consolidated, sometimes changed the order or even altered a word if clarity required it. Like any process of curating someone else's words, what to leave out was as important as what to keep. I chose not to include long, depressed ramblings that rehashed grief. I left in some rambling when he talked about gender confusion and about how to be strong and appropriate in a community, because he never resolved those things and continued to try to work them out.

Apples and Flamelight

p. 150. With visiting family and a lot of neighbors: On the tapes, he interrupts here, "Oh, my God! I'm just driving by something. There's a huge, huge pile of rocks that were on fire! Crazy. Really amazing sight to see. It's probably . . . I mean sixty to eighty—maybe a hundred feet wide. Uhhh . . . I'm on I-5 . . .

probably forty miles south of Stockton. I don't know what that was . . ."

p. 152. My father wanted me to be a well-rounded person, so he exposed me to writing and drawing and Aztec dance and then theater: I think I exposed him more to writing and drawing, while Cecilio brought him into Danza Azteca and theater. But until I moved to Washington, D.C. when Itzolin was eleven, both of us were involved as parents in his activities, even after we separated. We supported each other as much as we could, through the kids' back and forth between us.

p. 152. The clay pot that held the paint he painted me with when he baptized me: The tiny pots of black and red paint were not used to paint him, but I love that he felt it like that. They symbolized the way important stories were told in pre-Columbian languages. Glyphs (images) were essential to the telling. And Itzolin was such a teller, more than ever at the end of his life.

p. 153. I felt a tingling sensation over my whole body: Here he sings the lovely "Plaza Garibaldi" by [Enrique] Franco Aguilar. It's the one time in these audiotapes that he breaks into extended Spanish, and I really wanted to include it. He substituted two words, "darle" una serenata in place of *llevar/* "give" a serenata instead of bring it; and "querido" in place of *quedito/*"dear" instead of softly. My daughter Karina Marin identified this song for me, recognizing that on the clip of Itzolin's voice I sent her, his style resembled the much-loved group Los Tigres Del Norte, which has sung and recorded it numerous times.

In the course of finding out about quoting lyrics in a book, I fell into the amazingly complicated world of music copyrights, royalties, licensing and contracts. Fortunately, I was blessed with a few angels along the way. Please see the Acknowledgments page.

p. 156. There's something about rotten apple cores nearby me that I really liked: I asked Itzolin once why he constantly created this household chore for me, his mother, and he said thoughtfully that the smell entranced him!

p. 157. I stood up to him, although he was a lot bigger than me, and he body-slammed me: That day Itzolin came home from the Martineztown Center with bruises and a bleeding face. I complained to the staff, and the bully was called to account.

p. 158. And another time she got a black eye at preschool from some boy, in a struggle about a wagon, and she punched him and gave him a bloody nose: By all accounts, the boy hit Oraibi first.

Gifts of Desire and Respect

p. 160. . . . and working at the Southwest Network: SNEEJ, Southwest Network for Environmental and Economic Justice, Albuquerque.

p. 163. Mos Def CD that has "My Umi": It's "Umi Says," 1999.

The Fear and the Broken Sleep

p. 170. I made a large down payment: Throughout that year, I sent Itzolin fifty dollars a month. I didn't learn until recently that young Oraibi Karina sent him money, too.

p. 170. You've got a new car: Toward his end Oraibi Karina, twenty-three and working, secretly helped him again with occasional money. When he was about to lose the car, she even came through with the payment to save it. In his last documents he left it to her.

p. 171. There were things I had never talked about with anybody: After he came to live in San Francisco in 1992, I was able to get counseling for him through Victim Assistance. Eventually it was paid through a reparations program that made his imprisoned abuser accountable for payment. Itzolin declined to go to New Mexico to testify at the trial. Later some of the man's associates came to San Francisco, stalked him and tried to make him recant his original testimony. I then had a police officer come to our home, and Itzolin gave a full report about the harassment. His anxieties and trauma had already amplified before he went to Yale and then to graduate school. He seemed best with routine, discipline, artistic expression, and talking with family and friends.

p. 173. I don't know if it had something to do with medicine, 'cause I was taking Paxil and Trazodone: Both are anti-depressants. In May 2006, Glaxo-Kline sent a bulletin to prescribing physicians on changes to their Paxil labeling, WARNINGS section, Clinical Worsening and Suicide Risk subsection:
https://web.archive.org/web/20060616142401/http://www.fda.gov/medwatch/safety/2006/paroxetineDHCPMay06.pdf

Only There to Taste the Flower of Life

p. 174. Sometimes I would read at open mike at Locus: Itzolin became very much involved with Locus Arts, increasingly drawn to Asian-American writers, artists and musicians.

p. 174 – 175. I was leaning on things that were holding me up, but looking back on it, I wasn't carrying any of my weight: From October 2001 Itzolin regularly came over Saturday for Tejano-style family dinner. He'd then drive Oraibi Karina to evening church service in Daly City, with me tagging along in the car, come back to my place, share his work over tea, and tell me about his courses. He always had plans with friends later.

p. 175. I was literally a wanderer, carrying around my poncho and my bag: Stanford students say Itzolin sometimes arrived to class with a pot of food, sat down, and started eating it then and there.

p. 175. I've always been the kind of person that has to work hard at balancing the concrete things in life: In his last two years of high school before Yale, I worked with him to develop stable routines, keep his belongings in order, and manage his money, and he did. With the guidance of the Alta Program at McAteer High School, he became very focused on his plans for college.

p. 175. . . . but I was drinking so much, and I could: After Itzolin's death, I followed a formal process to retrieve his psychiatric records from Stanford. He had been counseled repeatedly about excessive alcohol use, especially since he was on medications, yet according to records, he insisted that it was fine and continued on this dangerous path. He was able to hide it from the family for a long time by drinking only when he was with friends.

Ocean of Clashing Shapes

p. 177 – 178. I've always had fear of people who have this power to make or break you: At nine or ten, Itzolin acted in a play where he wanted me to drop him off at rehearsals and pick him up after they finished. In Albuquerque it was normal for parents to stick around. Finally he told me white people weren't welcome there, and he'd be embarrassed for the cast to find out I'm not Latina. I told him that I'm his Mama—that's enough reason to be proud—and I'm going to come anyway. Also that I can handle myself in situations of mistrust or negative judgment. Though the director and cast members greeted me warmly, Itzolin remained convinced that they were putting on a show. He had fears of rejection for being half Scandinavian-American as well as Chicano. At times in college, he seemed under pressure to regard all white people as revolting imperialist scum. Conflicting loyalties tore at him.

Bridges

p. 180. Sometimes I would just eat brown rice or bread and bananas: At the time, he ate with Oraibi Karina and me at least once a week, but if he dropped in unexpectedly, he'd only accept a banana. When I noted that he looked pale, he said he had a rice cooker and was making himself hot food all the time. Sounds like he only used it for batches of brown rice!

p. 181. That word is from the Nahua *in xóchitl in cuicatl,* which means Flower and Song: Itzolin grew up with the early Chicano Floricanto celebrations of poetry and music, festivals that lasted for days in Austin, San Antonio, Houston and Arizona. He was there. Instead of tiring him out, these all-day, all-evening festivals delighted him, even as a baby.

Crazy Horse Rainbow

p. 183. Traditional instruments, like *el requinto jarocho:* A twangy, exceptionally soulful four- or five-stringed instrument of Veracruz, often made from cow horn, that plays bass lines in an ensemble.

p. 183. . . . or one of those little *tres* Cuban guitars: With origins in Guantánamo, the *tres* has its place at the heart of traditional Cuban music. There are many tunings, but it seems that A-D-F# is often favored in Cuba.

p. 185. Just last week I went to APAture and saw a lot of old friends: APAture 2002 Literary Event Evening, with Ishle Park and others, happened Friday, September 27, from 8 – 10pm. The Main Event took place Saturday, September 28, 2002 from 1 p.m. to 1 a.m., at San Francisco's SomArts Cultural Center, 934 Brannan Street. Some of his friends listed as performers included Annie Koh and Robynn Takayama. This schedule, no longer online, had appeared at http://www.apature.org/

Phoenix Hotel

p. 209. Zoquete: Colloquially, "clumsy oaf." Can also mean rind or scab. Here, in "Tlazolteotl Breakdance," it's Itzolin laughing at himself.

pp. *210* and *230.* Images by Oraibi Karina Marin are paño arte, a tradition of drawing on a handkerchief [pañuelo] or piece of cloth with ballpoint pen or colored pencil. Often called prison art, it appears to have started in western states with 1940s Mexican inmates who sent what they had created to family outside. Styles might come from murals, tattoos, graffiti, or magazines. Themes range from the Virgen de Guadalupe to Aztec warriors or Mexican heroes, from skulls and beasts to comic book figures. They're as simple and heartfelt or as figured and elaborate as the artist desires. The graceful, painstaking lettering style is highly embellished, like a medieval manuscript.

p. 212. Colita: Butt end, tail.

p. 219. The poster attributed to "Fortunio Archuleta" is part of the poem, in that it's from a drawing by Itzolin, which I found with his other drawings.

p. 221. Chamiza: A perennial herb, often planted as a hedge, that has white flowers with a yellow center. Its edible leaves are also used as a tea. The leaves can make a lather for itching or a poultice for ant bites. Chamiza is widely used and valued throughout New Mexico.

p. 236. Maquiladora: A foreign-owned factory in Mexico at which imported parts are assembled by lower-paid workers into products for export.
https://www.merriam-webster.com/dictionary/maquiladora
Retrieved January 27, 2021.

p. 242. Veladora: votive candle.

p. 244. Temazcal: From the Nahua term *temazcalli,* "house of heat," a circular Mexican sweat lodge where a curandera or shaman performs a traditional ritual for the sick. Herbs, sometimes hallucinogenic, may be part of this purification.

p. 245. Piñon: A common pine in the southwest, especially valued for its pine nuts.

p. 253. Paliacates: Bandanas in vibrant colors.

p. 261. Maborosi: Japanese, phantom or illusion of light. The visually compelling 1995 film of that name by Hirokazu Koreeda centers on the wife of a man killed by a train, when he inexplicably walks on its railroad tracks. Years later, as she suffers and questions why this happened, her second husband suggests that the other man may have felt haunted by a shimmering apparition that pulled him away from his life.

p. 269. Mahal kita: Tagalog, I love you.

p. 269. Saranghae: Korean, I love you (to someone you're close to.)

p. 269. Yollopoliuqui: Nahuatl, one whose heart has been lost, destroyed. Protection from "losing heart" (disturbances of mind and spirit) can come through the healing power of *yolloxochitl,* flower of the heart.

p. 270. Ahumador: Spanish, a small smoker oven.

Itzolin said, "Remember me beautiful."

285